THE GOSPEL IN GENESIS

'CHRIST IS ALL'

THE GOSPEL IN GENESIS

*

HENRY LAW

THE BANNER OF TRUTH TRUST

THE BANNER OF TRUTH TRUST
3 Murrayfield Road, Edinburgh EH 12 6EL

*

First published 1854
First Banner of Truth edition 1960
Reprinted 1961
Reprinted 1993

ISBN 0 85151 038 8

*

Printed and bound in Great Britain by
BPCC Paperbacks Ltd
Member of BPCC Ltd

PREFACE

THE object of these pages is simple, clear, holy. It is to arouse attention to the blessed truth, that Christ pervades all Scripture, as salt all waters of the sea, as light the brightest day, as fragrance the garden of choice flowers.

To see this is my prime delight. To testify it is my happiest duty. Devoted loyalty to Him who is the first and last, the sum and substance of all Scripture, impels me. Earnest zeal for the undying souls of men constrains me. I know, and am intensely persuaded, that all peace, all joy, all salvation, are in Him. My eyes are widely open to the fact that men are blessed, and are blessings, just in proportion as they live, ever gazing on Christ, ever listening to His voice.

Shame, then, and guilt and woe would be my portion, if I should leave any effort untried to unfold His glorious image. Let me rather use every power of life and pen to magnify and exalt Him:—to beseech men to ponder Him—to search for Him—to receive Him—to love Him —to follow Him—to serve Him—to commend Him—to live in Him, and through Him, and for Him. I would thus strive, the Spirit helping, to assail and melt and conquer hearts, that Christ may there be enthroned, in all His rightful majesty, a beloved and adored Lord.

There can be no excess in the faith and love and adoration and obedience of the only Saviour, the King of kings and Lord of lords. Has there ever lived the saint, whose moan it has not been, that, always striving to learn, he still was miserably ignorant in the full purpose of the Bible?

What is there comparable to the profit of this knowledge? It is helpful to men in everything, hurtful in nothing. Whatever be the station or employ, if the duties be performed with loving eye intent on Jesus, with mind rejoicing in His discovery, with heart luxuriating in His riches, then toil will be no toil, because of the constant refreshment.

Who will deny, that the happiest man on earth is he who is most enriched with enlightened views of Christ, and acts out most devotedly this faith? He lives at heaven's high gate. He holds close communion with Him, through whom his transgressions are forgiven, his sins are covered, his person accepted, his soul saved. He knows in whom he believes. He discerns the glories of His person, the redeeming worth of His wounds, the ransoming efficacy of the pierced hands and feet, the sheltering shadow of the cross. He reads the assuring language of Calvary. He sees his name written on the God-man's heart. To him the morning sweetly dawns, because it awakens to the renewed light of Jesus's grace. To him the day gladly speeds on, because its advance is progress in divine instruction. To him the night is calm repose, because he rests on the pillow of atoning love. The darkest cloud is fringed with rays of joy, while he meditates on salvation's Lord, and all events drop gladness.

Can I know this, and not beseech men to make Christ their All?

Till this be truly done, how dreary is the present state, and future prospect! Without Christ, religion is a sunless firmament; public service is a casket without jewel; life is a dreary passage to a dreadful end; the home is no abode of peace; the family has no strong bond of lasting love; the trade yields no returns of worthy profit; death is a downfall into unfathomable abyss; eternity prolongs unutterable woe. Without Christ, health is no healing of soul-sickness, and sickness is a prelude to immitigable pain. Without Christ, prosperity is an adverse tide, and adversity is a foreshadowing of deeper misery. Birth is no boon, if Christ be never born within. Life is no gain, except to live be Christ. Apart from Him, God is an adversary; Scripture sounds condemnation; Satan is waiting for his victim; his prison-house is ready to receive.

Can I know this, and not beseech men to make Christ their All?

We live, too, in days when countless fallacies court men in garb of truth. How shall we meet, expose, expel them? Wisdom is needed, for theologic error is shrewd and bold. It often is opposed by error, and then victory leaves darkness more dark. The conquering champion's panoply is full intelligence of Christ. Christ is the sword, before which Roman frauds and neologic sophistries fall low. He is the shield which guards the heart from all the poisoned arrows of the deceiving and deceived. In Him there is reply for every error's every wile. Christ truly seen is a fort impregnable. Christ well applied shivers all falsehood's armoury. He is God's wisdom in the highest. The man is safe on wisdom's high ground who is well versed in Him.

Therefore my desire in these pages is to turn minds to clear discoveries of their Lord. The Father's eye moves not from Him. The Spirit never wearies to reveal Him. Angelic intellect pants to dive more into His depths. The saints in light find Him increase of ever-lasting light. May the unfolding Spirit help each reader to glean more in the golden field of Scripture; and may the Pentateuch be found a boundless treasury of Christ!

HENRY LAW.

DEANERY, GLOUCESTER,
   27th October 1864.

CONTENTS

LIGHT

" God said, Let there be light: and there was light."
    —GEN. i. 3.

THE speaker is God. The time is before time was. The word is omnipotence. The result is the grandest of gifts. Darkness heard and vanished. "God said, Let there be light: and there was light."

Reader, strive to imagine the scene, when this first voice called this first blessing into being. This world of full delights was then one huge mass of unarranged material. It had no form, and therefore it had no beauty. It was vacancy, and vacancy wants all that pleases. It would have been cheerless, even if robed in cheering light. But impenetrable night shrouded the lifeless void.

From this rude quarry, however, the home of man is to be built. This waste is to be peopled with beings, whose age is immortality. It is to be the field, from which heaven's garner shall be stored. Therefore, deformity must assume form:—disorder must melt into order:—shapelessness must be shaped into loveliness.

How shall this be done?—God had but to will, and in one instant creation arises in full-blown perfection. But it is not so. He works by gradual process.—He works. Let us hence learn the wisdom and the need of effort. He works by gradual process. This teaches, that patient diligence is the path to all well-doing.

But what is the first wonder, which steps forth to usher in the train of harmony and grace? It is light. Do you ask what is the chamber of its birth? and what the art, by which it is composed? The reply is, "God said, Let there be light: and there was light."

To know more is impossible. And it is impossible, just because more knowledge would neither tend to profit nor to good. There are, however, truths linked with light, which are open to our earnest search. It is a casket rich in Gospel jewels. In its fair form we see the fairer features of the Lord of light. The Holy Spirit—no doubtful guide—proclaims, "That was the true light, which lighteth every man, which cometh into the world." Jesus, too, exalts it as His emblem, when He instructs, "I am the light of the world; he that followeth Me shall not walk in darkness, but shall have the light of life." The prophet, too, gazing on the rays of Christ, sings, "The people that walked in darkness have seen a great light." The apostle, intent on Jesus, exhorts, "Shew forth the praises of Him, who hath called you out of darkness into His marvellous light." We should close our eyes, then, on the high purposes of light, if we failed to trace therein the transcendent beauties of salvation's Dayspring.

Light is pure. In it there neither is, nor can be, mixture or pollution. Its property repels defilement. It traverses unstained each medium of uncleanness. Snow is brilliant;—no whiteness can surpass it. But man's step mars it.—Water sparkles brightly from its spring. Man's hand can soil it. But none can make light's purity less pure. Such is Christ. When man on earth, He was pure as God in heaven. He passed through a world of sin, as a sunbeam through the vilest hovel. He took indeed sin's form, that He might bear sin's due: but He never knew sin's stain. In Bethlehem's manger He was the holy Child. He returned to heaven in holy triumph, as the holy Conqueror.

Reader, study much the essential holiness of Jesus. It is one of the anchors of our Gospel-hope. He must be holy as God is holy, or He cannot mediate with God for us. If but a shadow of a sinful shade be on Him, atonement is needed for Himself: then He must save Himself: and we are left unsaved. But Jesus is all-sufficient to redeem us, because He is Jehovah's co-holy fellow.

Study it, too, as the model of the new-born soul. Salvation is conformity to His image, "He that hath this hope in Him, purifieth himself, even as He is pure."

Light is bright. Indeed, what is brightness but light's clear shining? The day is bright, when no clouds hide the sun. The prospect is bright, which reflects unnumbered rays. The hope is bright, which glitters free of foreboding gloom. Such is Christ. He is "the brightness of His Father's glory." He embodies, as in one constellation, every Divine perfection. He shines, the midday splendour of Jehovah's attributes. That time is the brightest time, in which the Lord is nearest. That page is the brightest page, in which most of Christ is found. That sermon is the brightest sermon, in which most of Christ is heard. That life is the brightest life, in which most of Christ is seen.

Light is lovely. Beauty cannot live without it. Exclude it, and every charm would hang a blighted head;— the sun would fade, and colour be extinct. Such is Christ. It is a true record, "Thou art fairer than the children of men "—" the chiefest among ten thousand—and altogether lovely." What fulness of beauty is in that person, who is God and man! what harmony of grace is in that work, which joins God to man! what charms are in those precious Scriptures, which shew His worth! To see His varied excellence is heaven begun. The sight makes earth a blank, and all its glories but a withered flower. Just, too, as lovely light makes lovely, so Christ decks all on whom His beams descend. He beautifies the meek with salvation.

Light is free. The wealth of the wealthy cannot purchase it. The skill of the skilful cannot frame it. The labours of the laborious cannot earn it. The poverty of the poor cannot debar from it. Wherever it comes, it flies on freedom's wings. It gilds the hall, unbribed by price. It illumines the hut, unbought by toil. Such is Christ.

Sinner, do you crave this precious treasure? Open the casement of the heart, and it is yours. "Come ye, buy wine and milk, without money and without price." Waste not then time in seeking a price for Him, compared with whom an angel's worth is nothing worth. All your fancied merits are only demerit. You best is sin, and will you offer sin for Christ? Plead misery and take mercy. Bewail darkness and He will give you light. All, who bask in His joyous rays, are one in this testimony. Each sings, My treasure is a free-grace gift: He loved me, because He would love me: He called me, because He would call me: He blessed me, because He would bless me: He saved me, because He would save me: He shone into my soul, because He would shine. When I was darkness, He said, "Let there be light: and there was light:" and the light was Himself.

Light is all-revealing. So long as darkness casts its mantle round, we move unconscious amid foes and mire. A pit gapes at our feet; an arrow is ready on the murderer's bow; each touch is a stain;—but we are heedless of our woe. Let the light dawn, then ruin and uncleanness stare us in the face. Such is Christ. By His rays, sin is detected, as lurking in every corner of the heart; and the world, which we so fondled, is unmasked, as a monster, whose embrace is filth, and in whose hand is the cup of death.

Reader, do you discern the defilement of sin, and the poison baits of the world? If not, light has not visited your conscience. Christ is not in your heart. In the lament of faith there is always this note, " Behold, I am black." In its mouth there is always this cry, " Wash me, and I shall be whiter than snow."

But as the sun is seen by its own light, so Christ reveals not perils only, but Himself. He shews His cross—the glorious proof of boundless love. He shews His blood —the precious payment of all debts. He discloses the treasures of His word. Then testimonies, and promises, and endearing calls, and soothing notes of comfort, start into brilliant life, as beauties in the sun-lit landscape. He draws back the curtains of His heavens, and we see a reconciled God, and catch the glimpses of a weight of glory.

Light is the parent of fruitfulness. Regions, which the sun rarely cheers, are barren wastes. In shade, vegetation languishes—trees droop. Perpetual winter is perpetual desolation. But mark the change, if genial warmth returns. The garden, the vineyard, the fields are soon clothed with fragrant and luxuriant plenty. Such is

Christ. In His absence the heart is rank with every weed, and every noxious berry. But when His gleams enliven, the seeds of grace bud forth, the tree of faith pours down its golden fruit.

Light is the chariot, which conveys heat. Without it, earth congeals into a rocky pavement. Our soil would be adamant, if our skies were black. So the heart without Christ is ice. But when He enters, a glow is kindled, which can never die. Love burns and blazes in every chamber of the inner man. This is the spark, which flares to heroism in the faithful minister and the toiling missionary. Christ seen and loved is warmth to the heart. Warmth in the heart is fire in the lips. Fire in the lips is a flame in the hearers. Thus hardened congregations melt into a flood of holy zeal.

Light, too, is the harbinger of joy. For three days Egypt was all blackness: sight failed and motion ceased. It was a dreary time.—In Paul's tempestuous voyage, for many days neither sun nor stars appeared. It was a dreary time.—But far more dreary is the Christless soul. Not until He lifts up His countenance can the happy morn begin, which has no night. Present light, however, is but the morning-star of coming glory. Here mists will sometimes rise. Heaven is a cloudless God. Then in bodies of light, and robes of light, the redeemed sit down in a city of light, " which hath no need of the sun neither of the moon to shine in it, for the glory of the Lord doth lighten it, and the Lamb is the light thereof."

Reader, are you journeying from light to light? Be not deceived. There is the taper of reason. This guides to no haven. There are the many false lights of error.

They delude to rocks, and quicksands, and whirlpools of destruction. Vain meteors glare from many pulpits, and in many books. The self-pleased votaries of forms and superstitions are dazzled by the tinsel of a fictitious cross. Beware! there is but one sun in the firmament. So there is but one Christ in the Bible—one Christ of the Spirit—one Christ of the Father—one Christ of the saved.

I ask again, Is your darkness passed away? It is so, if you see this one Sun of Righteousness, and hate sin, and crucify the flesh, and trample on the world. It is so, if you joy in His beams, thirsting for clearer knowledge, and a brighter path. But, perhaps, you love darkness rather than light, because your deeds are evil. Ah! think how fearful is the broad road! It goes straight down into the abyss, which is outer darkness, and where is weeping and gnashing of teeth for ever. Stay, I beseech you. Will you not turn to " the true light?"

Believer, you see the sunny spot, which is your home. In your full joy, remember, that this garden of the Lord is a place of work, and not of sleep. Your light is come, that you may arise and shine. You are light, that others may be light through you. Say not, it is not mine to create or to confer light. True; but it is yours to reflect it. The planet casts back rays. The mirror returns the image. The Christian shows forth Christ. Say not, I move among the blind. True; but your Sun gives sight as well as light. You saw nothing, until He said, See. Give Him no rest, until in your family, in your neighbourhood, in your country, throughout the world, His voice be heard, Let there be sight;—and there will be sight;—Let there be light; and there will be light.

ADAM

" The Lord God formed man of the dust of the ground."—Gen. ii. 7.

THE life of Adam is but a brief page. But each line supplies a volume larger than the books of human mind. We find in it the key of all, which amazes us in that marvel—Man. The countless now on earth—the countless in unutterable bliss—the countless in eternal woe—all hang on him as the parent-tree of being. All, who shall yet be born to shine in heaven or to glare in hell, must flow as streams from this fountain-head.

When we go back to the birth of him, who is this common birth, we naturally ask, of what material is the work? Pride would conclude, that no mean quarry could produce such frame. But pride must lie low before the unerring word, " Dust thou art."

Ponder this first truth. The mightiest monarch,—the Lazarus at his gate,—are one in base original. The common parentage is that of worms. The flesh of each is but the filth, which our feet scorn. Who, then, will boast of beauty or of strength? There is a voice in dust, which mocks such pitiable folly.

But man is more than a shell of clay. The mean case holds a matchless jewel. God " breathed into his nostrils the breath of life, and he became a living soul." The flesh is of the earth and earthy. The spirit is from on high and heavenly. One is the clog of matter. The other is a ray from God. One soon crumbles back to vileness. The other is a deathless principle. One sinks as to the level of the beasts. The other gives the wings of immortality.

Reader, you cannot think too highly of the soul. It cannot cease to be. Age after age imprints no wrinkle on it. It neither withers nor decays. Its time is time-less. Its death is never.

Thus man was formed. A lovely garden was the palace of creation's lord. Fragrance and fruit charmed and re-freshed each sense. Converse with God was the soul's easy flow. To live was unalloyed delight. The smile of innocence met the smile of heaven. The heart was only love:—the worship only praise.—But man was a creature, and a creature must obey. In heaven the angels do their Maker's bidding. God cannot be, except on a throne of rule. But obedience shall be no heavy yoke. Only one command is issued—one only tree forbidden. To transgress is death. "In the day that thou eatest thereof, thou shalt surely die." Who can hear this penalty, and think that sin is a trivial fault—easily to be pardoned—soon to be effaced? Nay! the slightest sin is the soul in open rebellion. It casts God from the heart. It strives to tread Him in the dust. It avows the godless principle of independence. It proves that self has erected the idol of self-love.

Can God then connive at evil? Ah! no. The whole of Deity abhors it. Therefore, to transgress is death. Such is the penalty. But who can fathom the depths of misery in this curse?—It involves the instant withdrawal of heavenly presence. It denounces withering to the core of every spiritual faculty and perception. It warns, that to rebel is to become death-stricken in body—dead in soul. It shows, that sin's proper home is the eternal gnawings of accusing conscience, and eternal tossings on the bed of wrath.

We now approach earth's darkest day. The tempter comes. We reason not with those who ask if this might not have been averted. We see that piety untried is piety uncertain.—With subtilty the snare is laid. Evil suggestion is presented. The first lie is muttered. Our parents pause to listen. Will they yield? Can they touch and taste? Alas! a perfect man is but a tottering reed. The one command is broken. Sin enters. Innocence expires. The life of God is extinguished in the soul. Adam hangs down his head, fallen and guilty, in a curse-doomed earth.

It becomes us to consider well the miseries of this foul deed. It is the clue of all the dark confusion, which perplexes us without, and humbles us within. The universe moves not on the pivot of right order. The brier, the thorn, the hard toil tell of a sterile soil. The storm, the hurricane, the earthquake, the blight, the pestilence, proclaim, that displeasure frowns from heaven. All things, by tending to decay, show, that death wields an unrelenting sceptre. The tears, the sighs, the groans, and all the train of sorrows, which follow in the rear of pain and bereavement, evidence that an angry God deals angrily. But this is not all. The bitterest curse fell on the heart. Alas! what a wilderness is it of hateful weeds! We read—and conscience echoes, it is true—" Every imagination of man's heart is only evil continually." "The Lord looked down from heaven upon the children of men, to see if there were any that did understand and seek God. They are all gone aside—they are altogether become filthy. There is none that doeth good, no, not one." The mind is vain—the understanding darkened —ignorance sits as guide—right feeling has fled. The creature is worshipped and served more than the Creator. The faithful Witness states it. All experiences confirm it. The records of the fall explain it. All woe came hand in hand with sin.

"In Adam all die." Reader, next mark, how it is, that all our race had share in the first sin. Adam stood before God, not as an isolated being, but as a common person. All generations were in his loins. The whole family of man were wrapt in that casket.—As one seed holds a forest; so all nations of all ages were involved in this one head. As all rays are in one sun; so all descendants were in this common stock. Thus Adam's act affects each latest child, as taint in the spring is taint in each issuing drop.

It follows, then, that in him we break the Covenant of Works. We sin in his sin. We offend in his offence. We transgress in his transgression. We are guilty in his guilt. In him we depart from God. In him we enter the cells of wrath. In him we put on the prison-garb of condemnation. In him we receive the heritage of curse. Will pride, which finds all elements of good in self, deride this statement? Let it first show why infants die —and why the first thoughts are buds of evil. There is no better proof of nature's blindness, than such flounderings in the mists and mire of unscriptural conceit.

To this point our view of Adam has been a cloud—gloomy, and scattering gloom. But look again. There

are bright rays behind. As we mourn, the Spirit flies
on wings of love to change the scene. Sweet voices cry,
Adam "is the figure of Him, that was to come," Rom.
v. 14. "The first man Adam was made a living soul.
The last Adam was made a quickening Spirit." I Cor.
xv. 45. "The first man is of the earth earthy. The
second man is the Lord from heaven." "As in Adam all
die, even so in Christ shall all be made alive." Blessed
tidings!—blessed privilege to trace the likeness! May
the Spirit help us now to look off from the sin-bringing
to the sin-bearing Adam!

Is Adam the parent of the whole family of nature?
So Christ is the parent of the whole family of grace. It
is written, " He shall see His seed." " A seed shall serve
Him." He is " the everlasting Father." As Adam is
the stock of corruption and of death; so Christ creates
anew to righteousness and life. He is a quickening
Spirit. As they that are born after the flesh are flesh; so
they that are thus born are spirit. Their powers, and
faculties, and perceptions are as light from darkness.
Once they were a mass of death. Now they have ears to
hear His call—and eyes to see His beauty—and mouths
to worship God and sing His praise—and hands to cling
to the cross—and feet to mount the hill of Zion. Once
their hearts were stone—now every pulse is love. Once
their taste was low and sordid as the earth—now they
are high and pure as heaven. The best of books is their
sweet pastime. The best of themes is their happy converse. New lineaments prove, that they are newborn.
Such is the happy progeny of grace. They sit in harmony around the table of Christ, and adore Him as the
author of their being, and their joy. Thus in Christ's

garden plants are made meet for the Paradise above—as in Adam's waste, weeds blacken for the burning.

But the contrast extends. Adam falls, and in him the world is cast down. Christ stands, and in Him all His seed lift up the head. He appears in flesh the common Head of His adopted. As such, He strides in triumph over every assault of Satan. As such, He moves in one unbroken, perfect course of pure and perfect love. God's fullest will is the one movement of His heart. His every member shares the victory and is righteous in the Righteousness. Thus each true believer boasts, "In the Lord have I righteousness:" and knocks at heaven's gate with the unanswerable plea. In Christ, my law-fulfilling surety, I bring the Righteousness of God. Great was the loss in Adam; but far greater is the gain in Christ.

So too, as a common person, He hangs upon the cross. In Him His people suffer unto death. In Him they exhaust the cup of wrath. In Him they taste the bitter pains, which sin deserved. In Him they pay the uttermost farthing into the scales of justice. In Him they endure, until each attribute of God requires no more. Thus each child of faith exclaims, with adoring praise, "I am crucified with Christ." Who can lay anything to the charge of one, who in Christ is discharged of all? In Adam we merit all wrath. In Christ we undergo it.

Christ rises from the dead. The icy bands cannot detain Him. But still he holds His people in Himself. In Him each sees an earnest of that resurrection-morn, in which this corruptible shall put on incorruption, and death shall be swallowed up in victory. In Adam we crumble in the grave. In Christ we find it the gate of

life. In Adam we lie down in beds of darkness. In
Christ we put on light as our robe for ever.

The work of redemption being ended, Jesus returns on
high. Does He ascend disconnected from His members?
Can the Head live apart? No. In Him they enter in
and take their seats before the throne of God. It is not
written without meaning or without truth, " He hath
raised us up together and made us sit together in heavenly
places in Christ Jesus." Every seat has been prepared
from everlasting ages: and in the view of God no seat is
vacant.

Do you say this is a mystery? It is.—But it is true as
deep. And it is revealed for the believer's comfort. For
what comfort like assurance of oneness with our Lord in
all which He has done, and is now doing? It is, too, the
seed of holiness; for who can dwell in spirit amid heaven's
glories, and touch the debasing vanities of earth?

Reader, it is a clear fact, that natural birth has brought
you into the old world of sin. How important the question, Has spiritual birth translated you into the new
world of grace? It is so, if you are Christ's:—and you are
Christ's, if Christ is yours;—and Christ is yours, if He
dwell in the heart by faith unfeigned: and faith is unfeigned, which ventures on Him, and ventures wholly—
which loves Him fully—which hears His voice and follows Him.

If this evidence be absent, you are still in a land of
ruin. And will you tarry a wretched wreck? Oh! cry
to Him, who always helps the helpless at their cry. Seek
life from Him, who is the Lord of life. Apply for quickening to Him, who is the quickening Spirit.

THE HEAVENLY BRIDEGROOM

" This is now bone of my bones, and flesh of my flesh."—GEN. ii. 23.

OUR Bible is a very Paradise of each sweet flower and each regaling fruit. But the believer sits down most gladly in those choice spots, which are thick-set with tokens of the Saviour's tenderness. Surely happiness mounts up to heaven, when on Scripture's ground, and under the Spirit's light, the soul discerns, that Jesus loves with an everlasting love.

Reader, this humble tract will visit you in a favoured hour, if it should lead you to drink deeply of such joy.

We cannot move far amid the pages of the Word, without hearing the silver voice, Give ear unto Me, that I may tell thee of My love. For this purpose each tender image speaks by turn. Does a father love with strength of manly love? Jesus is the Everlasting Father.—Is a mother gentle in her soft caressings? He is more constant: " they may forget, yet will I not forget thee."— Is a brother generous in his affections? He is the first-born among many brethren.—Is the sisterly union as the intertwining of hearts' fibres? The Church is " His sister, His spouse."—Is a friend noble in his sympathies? We read, " Henceforth I call you not servants—but I have called you friends."—Will not these parallels suffice? No: not if another can be added. As all colours combine to form pure light—so all tints must join to form the full portrait of a loving Saviour. There remains the full-blown endearment, when heart flows into heart in bridal union;—and will Jesus claim His people as His bride? It is so. This is the emblem, which is the Spirit's choice delight. It meets us in the garden of Eden. It walks by our side throughout the green pastures of the word. It only leaves us, when Revelation writes no more. "The Spirit and the Bride say Come." Echo replies to echo, "As the bridegroom rejoiceth over the bride, so shall they God rejoice over thee." "I will betroth thee unto Me for ever; yea, I will betroth thee unto me in righteousness, and in judgment, and in loving-kindness, and in mercies." Hos. ii. 19.

Following such holy guidance, let us now seek Jesus in that pure feeling, which innocently played in Adam's heart, before sin entered with unhallowing touch. The narrative is simple. "The Lord God caused a deep sleep to fall upon Adam, and he slept: and He took one of his ribs and closed up the flesh instead thereof; and the rib, which the Lord God had taken from man, made He a woman, and brought her unto the man." But the mystery is deep. A greater than Adam and the first spouse are in this history of sinless union. Faith has been taught, and quickly learns, that the spiritual Bridegroom and the mystic bride are here. Earth's first espousals are but the shadow of heaven's far earlier love. The second Adam sleeps a sleep—een the sleep of death; but not in Eden's innocent delights, but on the hard altar of His ignominious cross. His side is pierced. There flow thence the means to constitute the Church. There is blood to expiate every sin: and water to wash from every stain. The Father presents the bride to Adam. The same Father gives the favoured bride to Christ. Adam receives her as portion of himself. Christ's word takes up the same welcome. They "are members of His body, of His flesh, and of His bones."

We are thus emboldened to draw with reverential pen some lines of likeness. Marriage can only be in kindred race. Here the bride is low in lowly origin. Her coarse material is clay. But Jesus dwells in heaven's bright palace, bright in all the brightness, glorious in all the glories of His own Deity. How can union be? He leaves His home. He veils His Almighty might. He seeks our cell. He scorns not our loathsome rags. He is born a child of man in Bethlehem. He lives the Son of Man in human nature. O my soul! did your Lord thus stoop to make you His for ever? He did. Infinite was the distance: but He came with lightning-speed on wings of love—and rested not, until He rested in your far-off abode.

The bridegroom counts all efforts light to win the bride's regard. Can it be, that Jesus strives to gain unlovely souls? It is so. He lives, when we love. He scarcely seems to reign, until the heart presents her throne. Hence in the Scriptures He sends letter upon letter, each burning with the pure flame of tenderness. Hence He follows with the fond call, Turn ye, turn ye. Look unto me. Come unto Me. Return unto Me. Follow Me. Abide in Me. Hence He sends His faithful ministers—the friends of the Bridegroom—to plead His cause—to sue in His behalf—to beseech in His name—to set forth His matchless charms—to show that His love is strong as death, and pure as the light, and boundless as eternity.

That ministry is most true to Christ—most rich in
everlasting fruits, which paints most vividly the mind of
Christ.

But more than this. The Holy Spirit comes commissioned by the Father and the Son. He reveals the Lord
in all the beauties of His person—all the wonders of His
grace—all the glories of His work. He subdues all
prejudice—turns the stream of opposing will—and
kindles a blazing torch in the dark corners of the soul.
Thus union is achieved. The faithful soul forgets her
own people and her father's house. She casts out the
former rivals, which bewitched her thoughts. She comes
out and is separate from a once-fondled world. She leaves
all, and cleaves to Christ.

In nuptial bonds the bride rejects the distinction of
her former name. A new address attests, that she is no
more her own. It is just so in spiritual union. What!
though the style of Jesus proclaims essential Deity;—that
very style is the Church's diadem. Is it not so written
in Jer. xxiii. 6, and Jer. xxxiii. 16? We are first told,
that "The Lord our Righteousness" is His name. The
same is her portion, for it is added, "The Lord our
Righteousness" is her name too.

The bridegroom courts the closest communion. It is
even so with Jesus. By His Word, and through His mes-
sengers, He allures His people to His side. He opens to
them the purposes of His grace—the secrets of His kingdom. He encourages them to tell out their every want,
and fear, and desire, and hope. He tenderly invites,
"Let me see thy countenance, let me hear thy voice, for
sweet is thy voice, and thy countenance is comely."

Who can portray a bridegroom's sympathy? It is,

however, but a drop compared to the full ocean of a Saviour's care. "We have not an High Priest, who cannot be touched with the feeling of our infirmities." "He that toucheth you toucheth the very apple of His eye." "In all our affliction He is afflicted." No suffering member can be pained on earth, but the participating Head cries out in heaven, "Why persecutest thou Me?"

Reader, you have often heard these truths. Do they touch a responsive chord within? If not, yours is not the bride-like spirit.

The bridegroom brings his dowry. And does not Christ enrich with gifts? Angels may marvel, dazzled by the Church's wealth. He holds back nothing from her. All His attributes are her grand inheritance. His wisdom is hers to guide. His power is hers to uphold. His love is as the sun to cheer. His faithfulness and truth are her shield and buckler. His Spirit is poured down in unfailing measure to teach, to solace, and to bless her. His righteousness is hers, to be her spotless robe. His heavens are hers, to be her home. His throne is hers, to be her seat. His glory is hers, to be her crown. His eternity is hers, that she may joy for ever. Happy the soul, which responds, All this I steadfastly believe!

The bridegroom shrinks from no labours, which bring support and plenty to his beloved. Thus Jesus lives a life of watchful work. He rests not night and day. His outstretched hands are ever pleading, and ever pouring down supplies of grace. He purchased all Heaven's blessing, that His people may never want. And as each need arises, He is all vigilance to see—all bounty to bestow.

Earthly union often knows the pang of separation. Duty's stern voice may say, Depart. Necessity may force to lonely distance. But nothing in heaven, or earth, or hell, unlocks the arms which cling around a divine Bridegroom. At each moment He is nearer than the shadow to the side. Life is leaning on His arm. Death is sleeping on His breast. There is a never-failing bond in the sure world, "I will never leave thee nor forsake thee."

In this cold world affections cool. The day, which dawns in love, may close in hate. Tastes vary and cause variance. Discordant tempers make discordance. Far otherwise is the heavenly wedlock. It is ever true, "He that is joined to the Lord is one spirit." When Jesus calls in love, He changes by His spirit. He imparts a new nature, whose every pulse is unison with Himself. It is heaven's own harmony, when Christ is all.

Here a house is often tears, because of godless offspring. Many a one has sighed, "O Absalom, my son, my son!" But from heavenly union nothing springs but heavenly seed. Believers are married to Christ, that they should bring forth fruit unto God, Rom. vi. 22. Apart from Him, the heart is the hotbed of evil. United to Him, it is the holy parent of each holy grace.

But at present the Church sees her Bridegroom only by the eye of faith. The veil of flesh impedes the meridian gaze. But yet a little while and the day of manifest espousals will arrive. A startled universe will hear the shout, "Behold the Bridegroom cometh." There will resound, "as it were the voice of a great multitude, and as the voice of many waters, and as the voice of mighty thunderings, saying, Hallelujah, for the Lord God omnipotent reigneth. Let us be glad, and rejoice, and give honour to Him, for the marriage of the Lamb is come, and His wife hath made herself ready." Then shall He shine forth, "to be admired in His saints, and to be glorified in all them that believe." The bride "shall be brought unto the king in raiment of needle-work; with gladness and rejoicing shall they be brought, they shall enter into the king's palace." The nuptial song shall be one ceaseless Hallelujah. Happy soul, which responds, All this I confidently expect!

Reader, is it your happy privilege to know that a union, which thus lives for ever, cements your heart to Christ, and Christ to you? Remember, then, that this blessed relationship demands your faithfulness. The Lord is jealous of His people's love. You must not stray from Him for one single moment, or in one single thought. The caution is needful; for days are come, in which strangers are gone forth, professing to be the Bridegroom's friends. They even stand in pulpits, and give instruction in His name. By this sign you may know them. They exalt the bride rather than her Lord. They magnify His ordinances rather than Himself. They beguile her to admire herself, to lean on herself, to trust in herself, and to decorate herself in the mock robes of false humility and superstition. Take heed; the ground is slippery. It may seem pleasant to self-loving nature; but it slopes towards Antichrist.

It may be that some worldling reads this whose life is wedded to another lord. Would that such may turn and burst their fearful bonds! There is indeed the prince of this world. His promises are lies. His dowry is anguish. His embrace is death. His chamber is darkness. His bed is flames of fire. His marriage-wail is agony's wild shriek. Worldling, can you love this spouse?

THE SEED OF THE WOMAN

"I will put enmity between thee and the woman, and between thy seed and her seed: it shall bruise thy head, and thou shalt bruise his heel."
—GEN. iii. 15.

THESE are the first words of grace to a lost world. When were they spoken?—By whom?—To whom?

When? Just after sin had come in, and innocence was gone, and man had become a guilty creature before God. One command had been given, for the purpose of seeing whether he would love, and fear, and serve his Maker. That one command had just been trodden under foot.

Pause here for one moment and think. Some dream of earning eternal life by doing God's will. This way has been tried. It failed. The end of it was ruin. Our first parents were innocent, and had no inward movings towards evil, but they rushed into it. We are born with hearts corrupt, and fully bent on sin, and can we keep ourselves holy and spotless? It is a vain thought. Let us cast it away. We cannot continue blameless. Our wicked nature is always drawing us out of the straight path of godliness. We have not stood blameless during one hour of one day of our lives. The charge is true, and every honest conscience will confess it.

By whom were these words spoken? We read, "The Lord God said." What proof is here, that our God is merciful and gracious! Think how He had been offended! Think, with what base ingratitude,—with what contempt He had been treated! Satan's lie had been trusted rather than His truth. His easy yoke had been broken, as if it had been some hard restraint. The language of the proud heart had been, We will not have our God to reign over us.

God, even He, descends. No thunder-bolt is in His hands. No avenging angels follow to sweep the rebels into perdition. The voice which speaks is the voice of mercy. The tidings, which are brought, are the tidings of deliverance.

O my soul, can you consider the Speaker, and not exclaim, Truly, God is good: He willeth not the death of a sinner! Reason as the wife of Manoah did, " If the Lord were pleased to kill us, He would not, as at this time, have told us such things as these," Judges xiii. 23.

To whom were these words spoken? Three only were present. First the guilty pair. Mark their state: and learn from it that the first step in the way of salvation is taken by God. We have sure evidence before us. He wills to save, when man wills to die. He moves to save, when man moves to perish. Our first parents are before Him, a picture of all fallen sinners who should be born of them. As they were, so are we by nature. They were sinners, blind and hardened. So are we. Blind, I say;— for their eyes were not opened to the awful condition into which they had passed, or the awful misery, which was now their lot. Hardened, I say;—for they did not confess their sin, or humble themselves, or weep tears of sorrow, or utter prayers for mercy. Just such is man's natural blindness and hardness from that day to this.

And still to such God comes in love: to such God speaks of recovery to His favour and His kingdom.

Reader, calmly meditate on this. You will see, that when man is all careless, God is all care; when man can do nothing, God does all; when man deserves nothing, God gives all. Salvation is from first to last of grace. Man rushes to hell. Grace calls to heaven.

Next, another being was present. But there was no hope for him. He was only told, that destruction was his doom. We have here a proof, that God makes a difference between offenders. Let us not vainly ask, why mercy yearns over man, and turns from the angels which fell? There can be but one reply, " Even so, Father, for so it seemed good in Thy sight." And can we so reply, and not sing praise, that we, who have so sinned, should be so pitied, and have such rich provision of pardon? O my soul, think on these things.

But what is this rich provision? We read the answer in the word, " her seed." Here is a promise, that a deliverer should come into this world, who should be born of a woman. If the question be put, " Who is this seed of the woman?" we readily reply—The Lord Jesus Christ. The blessed Saviour. The only Redeemer. The only begotten Son of God Most High. True—The voice of God here promises that Jesus, appointed to save—should be made man,—should be one of our family by birth,— should be bone of our bones, flesh of our flesh.

The fact is easily stated. But, reader, is it your habit to ponder over the great and precious truths belonging to it? Mark! The mighty God, without ceasing to be God, becomes man to redeem us. Wonder of wonders! The like to this never has been—never could be. Let the greatest king become the meanest beggar:—let the richest prince leave his palace for the vilest cell of a loathsome prison; it is as nothing to the act of Jesus, when He left heaven to put on Him the rags of our mortality. The Creator of all things appears a creature! The Almighty is a weak babe!—The Eternal is a child of time!—The Infinite is contracted into the limits of this poor flesh! Is not this the wonder of wonders? Is not this grace which has no bounds? Reader, do you seriously believe, that Jesus thus humbled Himself even for you? If you do, you cannot but feel, that no debt can be like your debt; and that, as heaven is high above the earth, so great is what you owe, beyond what you can ever pay.

In the poor matters of this earth, a prince's or a noble's birth awakens signs of far-extending joy. The banners wave. The steeples sound. The festive board is spread. Shall we then call upon the realm of nature to celebrate with worthy praise this praise-surpassing fact? What! if the sun could hang forth millions of lamps, each brighter in brilliance than itself; what! if each drop of ocean's water could raise a chorus of ecstatic hallelujahs; what! if each leaf of every forest could cast back the pealing shout; it would be shame to offer a tribute so unfit.

But there is a testimony of delight which Jesus seeks. He is repaid, when grateful hearts throw wide their portals to receive Him, and when welcoming praise extols His saving name. O my soul, will you not then bid all that is within you, to clap the hands of loving worship around the manger at Bethlehem?

When Abraham saw the day of Christ afar off, he re-joiced and was glad. The unborn Baptist could not restrain emotion, when the unborn Jesus was brought near.

The beacon-star filled the journeying sages with exceeding great joy. The multitude of the heavenly host, who shared not in redemption's mercies, made heaven's vault to echo with their praises. O my soul, can you be silent? Hear you not the angel's cry? "I bring you good tidings of great joy." Will you not with great joy drink in these tidings? "Unto you is born a Saviour, which is Christ the Lord." Will you not, in aged Simeon's spirit, clasp Him to the heart of faith, and lift up the hymn of praise?

Next, have you, too, seriously pondered for what exact object Jesus became the Woman's Seed?—Our peace and happiness depend on the right knowledge of this. It was just for this purpose, that He might be qualified to stand in the poor sinner's stead; and might be in a condition to represent him. You know, that the Word of God has passed, and cannot be called back: "The soul that sinneth, it shall die." You know, too, that to die, in this sentence, means to suffer for ever the torments of the lost. Under this condemnation you and I are brought by sin. You and I, then, must thus endure, unless God be pleased to take the death of a sinless one in the place of our death. Jesus is willing to bear all for us: how could He do so, without being man? He could not. Therefore, He is made man. So when God's Truth and Justice say,—I must have that man's life; Jesus is ready to reply,—I am of his nature, here is my life for his. Mark, then, He is the Woman's Seed, that He may have a life to lay down, and have blood to shed, for the ransom of such as we are. See clearly, that Jesus takes man's flesh, that He may redeem from death all of man's family who trust in Him.

Thus, also, in man's nature, He obeys all the commandments of God. But the righteousness thus worked out is not for Himself. It is wrought, that He may make it over to all who come to Him. This He never fails to do. So when the poorest believer presents himself for admission into heaven, he can shew, for his passport, a perfect righteousness placed over him by Jesus. It is so all-sufficient, that, when weighed in the balances of God, it lacks nothing.

I repeat these truths, because they are the groundwork of true faith. Jesus was the Woman's Seed, that, being exactly as we are, yet without sin, His death might go for our death,—His righteousness might stand for our righteousness.

Reader, are you a poor sinner, feeling your misery and dreading eternal wrath? Flee to the Woman's Seed. There is pardon in Him to wash away all iniquities. The faithful of the old world knew Him by no other name, but they believed God, that, in due time, He would come, and thus satisfy for them. They looked to Him who should be born. They looked, and none can look in vain.

Do you seek after a righteousness to make you fit to appear in heaven? It is all ready in the Woman's Seed. Stretch out the hand of faith,—take it, and it is yours for ever. Whatever you need dwells richly in the Woman's Seed. Cast on Him your vileness, and take His purity; cast on Him your poverty, and take His riches; cast on Him your nothingness, and take His fulness; cast on Him your curse, and receive His blessing.

Do you hesitate—do you stagger—fearful to approach one so excellent in holiness? Well might you tremble, if bade to draw near to God in His glory. But He, who calls you, is your Kinsman—the Woman's Seed.

You may fly up to Him on the wings of faith, and embrace Him with the arms of faith, and cling to Him with the hands of faith, and lay your weary head upon His breast, and tell Him all your sorrows; and you will find that His heart is a brother's heart, as tender to compassionate as His power is all-sufficient to save.

Do you still stand doubting? What, when Jesus has come so far for you, will you not stir one step towards Him? When He has stooped so low, will you not ascend to Him? When He brings Himself, in man's form, to your very door, will you not open and welcome Him? Surely there is enough in the Woman's Seed to slay all unbelief; enough to win and conquer every heart. Here we see heaven coming down to earth, that earth may be raised to heaven. Here we see the Son of God becoming man, that men may become the children of God. Will not this satisfy—persuade—allure? Surely God could do no more. Man, then, can say no more.

I close with this earnest entreaty; read these few words again and again, until you find the flame of faith and love kindling in your soul; and then, on the bended knees of gratitude, exclaim, I bless Thee, Heavenly Father, for the promise in Eden of the Woman's Seed. I bless Thee, for sending, in the fulness of time, the Woman's Seed. I bless Thee, O Lord Jesus Christ, for coming to save me, as the Woman's Seed. I bless Thee, Holy Spirit, for revealing to my soul the Woman's Seed.

THE SERPENT'S HEAD BRUISED

*"I will put enmity between thee and the woman,
and between thy seed and her seed: it shall
bruise thy head, and thou shalt bruise his heel."*
—GEN. iii. 15.

WE look around us, and we see the world full of sin.
We look within us, and we find hearts full of the
same sad plague. It is a terrible fact;—and we ask with
a sigh, how did evil gain this rule? God's word only can
give the answer. We there read, that one in the form of
a serpent enticed our first parents, and, by prevailing,
changed their nature.

But who is this serpent? We further learn, that it is
the devil.—He thus disguised himself, that he might de-
ceive. The Bible does not close, until this truth is left
beyond a doubt. It is twice written, "that old serpent,
which is the Devil and Satan," Rev. xii. 9, xx. 2. The
moving cause, then, of our being born in sin, and living
in sin, stands confessed.—It is the Devil.

He obtained his first power over our race by deceiving.
He continues that power by deceiving still. His main
art is to keep us blind concerning himself, and concerning the great Deliverer. I am sure of this, because I see
many, who pass all their days without one real thought,
that they have a foe always near, plotting their misery.
They hear and perhaps speak of him, as though he were
an empty name, and not a mighty and most malignant

power. Reader, this may be your case. If so, turn not, I humbly implore you, from a few words, which, by God's grace, may be light to your darkness, and life to your captive soul.

Consider his nature. His titles shew it. He is the prince of this world, John xii. 31. Therefore his sway is world-wide. All the millions of our race, without one exception, were born his bond-slaves. They entered life with his chains around their hands, and with his throne erected in their hearts. Can they gain freedom for themselves? No. His guards are too many and his fetters too strong. Do they desire it? No. The will, by nature, chooses his service. Jesus warns, " Ye are of your father the Devil, and the lusts of your father ye will do," John viii. 44.

He is the god of this world, 2 Cor. iv. 4. He sets up the idol of fame, or pleasure, or money; and men fall down and worship it. He opens his temples, and decks them with attractive show, and ministers therein a pleasing cup of error, and multitudes go in to learn his creed.

He is leader of countless troops. There is not a spot—a house—in all the world, which he leaves unoccupied. Do we go forth? we are surrounded. Do we seek solitude? we are followed. In the courts of God—in the place of concourse—his vassals swarm around us. We read of a legion in one person. How vast then must be the collected army! Hence there is a sense in which ubiquity is his; because there is no place, which some of his emissaries do not fill. So, too, omniscience may be claimed for him; because there is nothing, which some ear does not hear for him. Whatever be our acts, he beholds; whatever be our words, he hears.

He is a spirit, Eph. ii. 2. Therefore he has access to the secret places of the heart. He can plant the seeds of all evil in the mind. If we close the outward gates of sense, he can still come in, and defile the thoughts, and make every imagination as wicked as himself.

He entered into Judas Iscariot, Luke xxii. 3. He filled the heart of Ananias, Acts v. 3. Reader, has he not often made lodgment within you? Oh! think, then, why is not your lodgment among his slain ones!

He is as crafty as he is strong. His real design is seldom known, until his bait is taken. His web is not seen, until the victim is entangled. The hidden pit is only discovered by the fall. He has been employed in the same employ for nearly six thousand years. Therefore he well understands his tools, and the materials on which he works. He is studying our tempers and characters all the day long. We know little of ourselves;—he knows us perfectly. He sees the weak point—the fitting time—and accordingly he lays the snare.

Gehazi little thought that Naaman's visit would be the tempter's trap. Hezekiah as little thought that the embassage from Babylon would unmask his vain-glory. A question from a servant girl in a moment plunges Peter into cowardly guilt. Reader, ever watch, ever pray, if you would escape temptation.

This is a dark picture. Who can view it, and not tremble? But, though fearful, it is only a faint outline of the mighty and cruel enemy of souls.

Give ear now to the tidings which I proceed to proclaim. Though he is strong, there is one far stronger. Though he is great, there is one gloriously greater. Though he is mighty, there is one Almighty. Though he is wily, there is one All-wisdom. Though he is many, there is one Infinite. Though he is a captivator, he has been taken captive. Though he is an enslaver, he has become a slave. Though he forges chains, he is enchained. Though he has brought low, he lies low. Though he is a conqueror, he has been conquered. The blessed Jesus comes a Conqueror, a Deliverer, a Redeemer, a Saviour. He treads down the devil, and gives deliverance, redemption, salvation to all the children of men, who stand under His banner of victory.

Reader, perhaps you are one of anxious spirit, and are not ignorant of many tremblings, lest at last you should perish by the hands of this foe. If so, how eagerly you will say, Give me proof that Jesus crushes this tyrant's power. All praise be to the God of grace! proofs abound.

Listen to the voice of the Lord God in Eden. "It," the Seed of the Woman, the Lord Jesus, "shall bruise thy head." Did not God know what should be? He did.— Can God speak, and His word not come to pass? Impossible.—Then this fact is true;—the serpent's head must be bruised by Jesus. Take comfort, then; take courage. Man was scarcely ruined, when he, who ruined him, was doomed to ruin. The savage joy of having marred creation's beauty was only felt, to be turned into the writhings of hopeless rage. Success was despair. He removed his foot from the neck of fallen man, and fled from the garden with the undying sound echoing in his ears, " It shall bruise thy head."

Such was the sure sentence of God. Now take a case which shows, that Satan's power has indeed a power above it.

You know the story of Abel. He trod this earth a

fallen being, as we are: hated by Satan, as we are: exposed to all his wiles, as we are. But he trusted in the promised seed for escape, Satan could not hold him. His early death, by a murderer's hand, landed him not in the kingdom of hell but of God. Thus the first soul, which left a human body, proved, that Jesus could rescue the prey out of the destroyer's jaws.

You know, too, the story of Enoch. He was a man of like nature with us,—born in corruption. You cannot doubt, that Satan shot his every arrow at him. But his soul received no fatal wound. It was guarded by faith in the coming Saviour. By faith in this promise he walked with God. By faith he mounted to heaven,—another jewel in the Conqueror's crown.

In the same way, all the holy men of the old world found that there was shelter and safety under the wing of the promised Conqueror. One promise convinced them, and gave them life. How many testimonies tell you of this rescue! Oh, let them not teach in vain!

But, in fulness of time, the Conqueror appears in human form. Satan knows him well. He heard the voice from heaven, "This is my beloved Son, in whom I am well pleased." He makes one desperate effort to obtain the mastery. The blessed Jesus meets the conflict. Every advantage of outward circumstance is given to the adversary. He draws from his quiver his oft-tried and most successful darts. He musters his strength and all his skill. His empire depends on the issue. The most that hell can do, is done. But all in vain. Each blow falls harmless before the Word of the Lord. The devil quits the field, baffled and beaten. He finds himself held down by the chain, "It shall bruise thy head."

He makes one effort more. He stirs up wicked men to seize and nail the blessed Jesus to the cross. When the Woman's Seed bows His head and dies; the enemy seems to triumph. But the end of the combat shews where the victory is. If Satan is the stronger, let him keep Jesus in the grave; let the prison detain the prisoner. But it does not—it cannot. Jesus bursts the doors;—comes again from the dead;—shews Himself alive;—and ascends in triumph to the heavens. Thus the victory is for ever won. The destroyer lies for ever destroyed beneath His feet. And when a few more years are past, the Lord Himself shall descend from heaven with power and great glory, and the devil shall be cast into the lake of fire and brimstone, and shall be tormented day and night for ever and ever, Rev. xx. 10. There is everlasting fire prepared for the devil and his angels, Matt. xxv. 41. "It shall bruise thy head."

The point, then, is clear. God is true. Jesus is Conqueror. The Goliath of hell is fallen.

Reader, this battle has been fought, this victory won, that poor sinners may be rescued. May the Holy Spirit help you to behold your high tower of safety, and to flee into it! Satan cannot but hate you,—for his name is hatred, as surely as God is love; and he desires to have you, that he may sift you as wheat. But if you are found in Jesus, you are high above his reach. He will attack. He will threaten. He will affright.—But Jesus will be your shield; and that shield must be shivered before you can be harmed.

Study the records of the Word. It is the history of the long war between the children of light and "the power of darkness." You will see, that he has tried every weapon of the armoury of hell. He has no other in reserve. But all have failed. They cannot rise higher than the heel. The head is safe with Christ in God. Mark, too, how a mightier hand guides his blows to wound himself. Satan's kingdom is made to totter under Satan's assaults. He brought in sin, and so the door flew open for the Gospel. He persecutes the early converts: and the truth spreads rapidly abroad throughout the world. He casts Paul into the dungeon of Philippi: and the jailor believes with all his house. He sends him a prisoner to Rome, and epistles gain wings to teach and comfort all the ages of the Church.

Fear not, then, believer, the curse is on your foe. Dust is his food. He cannot swallow the jewels of Christ's crown.

He may entice you with many things sweet to sense; but look to the Cross, and you see them no more. He may terrify you with roarings, as of a lion; shew him the wounds of the Lamb, and he is gone. He may stand as your accuser at the judgment seat; but if you are washed in the blood of Jesus, he can find no mark in you, by which to claim you as his own. Be assured, if you are one with Jesus by faith, His full triumph is yours, "and the God of peace shall bruise Satan under your feet shortly." If such be your happy case, lift up your head with joy and sing the holy song, "Thy right hand, O Lord, is become glorious in power: Thy right hand, O Lord, hath dashed in pieces the enemy. And in the greatness of Thine excellency, Thou hast overthrown them that rose up against Thee: Thou sentest forth Thy wrath, which consumed them as stubble," Exodus xv. 6, 7.

THE GUILTY CLOTHED

" *Unto Adam also, and to his wife, did the Lord God make coats of skins, and clothed them.*"—GEN. iii. 21.

THERE is one God and one access to His smile. There is one heaven and one door to it. The Saviour, who was to come, and the Saviour, who is to come, is one Christ. The faith of Abel and of the Baptist looked to the same object. Noah did not preach one righteousness, Paul another. The Patriarchs did not rejoice in one hope, the Apostles in another. From first to last, all the pilgrims to the hill of Zion lean on one arm.—All the voyagers, who cross the sea of life to the haven of eternal rest, are guided by one compass.

How all-important, then, is the thought for you, for me,—Have we escaped the many by-roads of destruction? Are we securely journeying along the one only track which leads to life?

The Lord Jesus Christ is this one way.

The rays of His redeeming love burst forth, so soon as there was a sinner to be enlightened. The garden of Eden witnessed the dark sight of innocence destroyed;— but it witnessed, too, an earnest of more than innocence restored. The parents of our race were not driven into the wide wilderness of the earth without a cheering prospect, and a strong comfort, and a precious promise, and a distinct figure of full recovery. The heavenward road

46

was marked out before them in a clear map. Jesus was pictured to them in living colours.

Even the clothing made for them, and put upon them, preached the Gospel to them. Consider their case.—They were conscious of shame, and blushed to meet the light of day. In their distress they sought concealment. They contrived—human invention could do no more—a shadow of a raiment. How flimsy, how tattered was it! But God in mercy came to their relief. He supplied all their need. He made " coats of skins and clothed them."

It may be that hitherto you have seen nothing in these garments but a warmth for the body and a screen from the blast. But be assured, the meaning is far larger. It is spiritual. It tells us of the robe of Righteousness, which God has provided to adorn and beautify the naked soul. May the Lord, by His Spirit, show this wonder to us!

We gain light on the subject by examining the substance of which the coats were made. It was not leaves joined together,—nor twisted bark,—nor plaited roots. It was the skin of lifeless animals. Death, then, must have commenced its desolating work within the garden. But how did it approach its earliest victims? Not in the slow step of gradual decay. This was the morning of existence. Time was in its infancy. The wastings of age were yet far off. These beasts of the field must have fallen by the hand of violence.

But why? Not to supply man with food. Before the flood, herbs alone sufficed for nourishment. Noah was the first who heard the enlarged grant, " Every moving thing that liveth shall be meat for you; even as the green herb have I given you all things," Gen. ix. 3. They were slain, then, for some other purpose.

It could have been no unholy purpose, for God regarded their slaughter with no displeasure. This He testified by using their skins. If, then, they died according to the will of God, but not to feed man, there remains only the solid conclusion, that they were offered in sacrifice. Thus they exhibited the Lamb " foreordained before the foundation of the world." And hence we learn that in Eden victims bled. Yes! the first drop, which stained the earth, the first expiring groan, proclaimed in the most intelligible terms, " the wages of sin is death;" and "without shedding of blood is no remission." The doctrine of these rites is the doctrine of the Cross.

All doubt is thus removed as to the skins, which supplied man's first apparel. They were taken from the offerings for sin. Hence each sacrifice presents to the eye of faith the double sign of full salvation. Each altar casts a shadow, not only of the blood, which buys from hell; but also of the Righteousness, which buys all heaven.

Such is the figure.—It is indeed admirable for simplicity. But who can express the length and breadth of the truth, which it unfolds?—a truth, which is the very key of heaven, and the green pasture of the soul. Until we understand this, we are only at the threshold of the Gospel. Will you not, then, draw nearer with me to seek the full comfort of full knowledge?

I cannot doubt that your earnest desire is, when this short life is past, to enter into the joyous mansions of the blest. But have you robes of your own fit for such abode? To be in heaven is to be with God. All there are beauteous in holiness. All shine in purity. All are white in spotless perfection. The eye of God rests on each with delight. He can find no blemish in them. He counts them all meet to sit on thrones of glory. But how have they obtained this unsullied raiment? It can be nothing framed by man. Defiled hands can only work defilement. "We are all as an unclean thing, and all our righteousnesses are as filthy rags." It is plain, then, that if we could dwell where nothing but Righteousness reigns, we must bring Righteousness with us. It is equally plain, that we can as easily make ourselves gods, as array ourselves in unstained robes. Who then will deck us, that we may be found worthy?

This reasoning leads us to the glad tidings of the glorious Gospel. All is provided for us in the Saviour Jesus. The Righteousness needed by us, and presented to us, is His obedience. He does for us, what we could never have done. In Him we become what we never could have been without Him. He works out an infinite worthiness, that He may be to us all that His name imports, "The Lord our Righteousness."

How precious is this well of truth!—Let us draw deeper refreshment from it in gratitude and faith. Behold again and again the glorious fact. One, made of a woman, has passed through human life without once straying from the path of God. The earth has seen a man pure as God is pure, holy as God is holy, perfect as God is perfect, sinless as God is sinless. He went round the circumference of the law without one deviating step. With strong wing He soared to its utmost height, and neither paused nor flagged. The searching eye of God always upon Him, could not once find the

absence of heavenly love in any thought, or word, or
deed. He had all trials, but no fault;—all temptations,
but no sin. The ground was ofttimes slippery, but He
never slipped. He was assailed on all sides, but He never
fell.—Thus He stood before God, holding in His hands
a full unbroken obedience,—accomplished,—completed
to the minutest letter. But it was all for us. He wrought
it, that He might give it; and He gives it to every naked
sinner, who in faith flees to be thus sheltered by Him.

Reader, perhaps you eagerly exclaim, Are these tidings
confirmed to me by the mouth of the Lord? They are.
They are. Listen to His words: "The Righteousness of
God, which is by faith of Jesus Christ unto all, and
upon all them that believe," Rom. iii. 22. Fully trust
this saying. and all peace is yours. It is "unto all," as
payment placed to their credit in the book of account.
Thus when God reckons with the believer, and asks the
fulfilment of the law, behold! there appears on his behalf, deposited by the hand of Christ, an obedience ex-
tensive with the very uttermost demand. God neither
desires nor can receive more. So, too, it is "upon all."
Hence, when the believer stands at heaven's gate, he
appears in heavenly robes.—The righteousness of Christ
is upon him. What more can be required? It is as
bright and glorious as God Himself.

I would, indeed, that you should be satisfied on this
point. In this affectionate desire, I beseech you to
weigh well another Scripture: "He hath made Him to
be sin for us, who knew no sin, that we might be made
the Righteousness of God in Him," 2 Cor. v. 21. Blessed
is the man in whose heart these words take root! They
are precious beyond ten thousand times ten thousand

worlds. Do not they state that we,—even we,—who are all vileness by sin, if only we are one with Christ by faith, are made the Righteousness of God! To be reckoned righteous would be much. To be made Divine Righteousness is far more. O my soul! limit not this mercy. Rejoice in the full comfort. The humble believer re-echoes Scripture, when he says, I am made in Christ the Righteousness of God.

It is manifestly the Lord's will, that this provision for the soul should be always present to our adoring eye. Therefore it is, that the object most familiar to our senses—even the covering of the body,—is planned to portray it. Study, then, this lesson. It is suited to every mind. The palace and the cottage alike teach it. It is as clear to the unlettered as to the learned.

I would fain commend it to your faith and your affection; but I find that earthly shadows fall as far short of the heavenly reality, as the creature is nothing when compared with the Creator.

We admire Adam's robe of innocence. It was pure and lovely, but it was human. Not so this robe. It is Divine. The God-man, Jesus, is its Author. Adam's robe was soon soiled and lost. Satan touched it, and it crumbled into nothingness. This is kept in the height of heaven; the destroyer cannot reach it. The skins brought to Adam would soon wax old, and perish. This is "everlasting Righteousness," Dan. ix. 24. Age rolling after age brings no decay; its newness is unfading. Earthly robes are sometimes of surpassing splendour. But what would be the brightness of Solomon's royal apparel beside this?—dim as the fairest star before the sun in mid-day strength.

Here I stop, feeling that eternity cannot exhaust the praises of this garment. But I have not written in vain, if these few words make its preciousness more precious to the souls of any.

Reader, do you desire to possess it? Ask, and you have. Seek with earnest faith, and it is yours. The prodigal returns, and the father says, "Bring forth the best robe and put it on him," Luke xv. 22. The weeping penitent comes, and heaven's best robe is cast around him. Be wise, then, and listen to the voice, which cries from above, "I counsel thee to buy of Me—white raiment, that thou mayest be clothed."

What can you desire more? Here is Christ's worthiness, for our unworthiness.—His sinlessness, for our sinfulness.—His purity, for our impurity.—His beauty, for our deformity.—His sincerity, for our guile.—His truth, for our falsehoods.—His meekness, for our pride.—His constancy, for our backsliding.—His love, for our hate. —In a word, His fulness, for our emptiness.—His glory, for our shame.—His one Righteousness, for our manifold unrighteousness.

Happy the man, who replies, I hide myself in Thee, O blessed Jesus! I receive Thee, as of God made unto me Righteousness.—He sweetly sings, "I will greatly rejoice in the Lord, my soul shall be joyful in my God; for He hath clothed me with the garments of salvation, He hath covered me with the robe of Righteousness," Isaiah lxi. 10. He humbly adds the note of transport, "Henceforth there is laid up for me a crown of Righteousness, which the Lord, the Righteous Judge, shall give me, at that day; and not to me only, but unto all them also that love His appearing," 2 Tim. iv. 8.

THE MORE EXCELLENT SACRIFICE

" *Abel, he also brought of the firstlings of his flock,
and of the fat thereof.   And the Lord had respect unto Abel and to his offering.*"—GEN. iv. 4.

ALONG course of years has fled, since the earth drank
in the blood of Abel. His was the earliest of all
graves. But he is not silent in it. His faith has an ever-
living voice. No time can stop its warning sound. " By
it, he, being dead, yet speaketh," Heb. xi. 4.

Such is the heaven-told fact.—Surely then there must
be much most worthy of notice in his testimony, since it
thus rolls on from age to age. Its subjects must be all-
important. It is so: —none can be compared to it. It is
so: —for it proclaims the Lord Jesus Christ.

This is the purport of its call to every child of man,
" Believe on the Lord Jesus Christ and thou shalt be
saved."—Trust in His blood.—Plead nothing but His
death before God. Make His cross your only hope.

Reader, perhaps you have never found all this Gospel
in Abel's brief life. But it is there. Unfold with me the
record: and let us do so in humble prayer, that the Spirit
may graciously teach. For without His aid, none ever see
the Lord.

Abel stands before us in the lovely character of one
whose spirit rejoices in God his Saviour. This is the
prominent feature in his portrait. He selects the first-
born of his flock. He brings it as an offering.—He lays

it on the altar.—He raises the knife.—He takes the life, as a debt due to God.

Such is his conduct. But what moves him to this mode of worship? He must have some grand intent. Let us trace it.

Did reason convince him that he was a sinner, and shew him that, as such, his own life was forfeited? Did it whisper the hope, that he might recover it, by giving another in its place? Did it suggest the idea, that the death of a guiltless victim might be the release of a guilty soul? That could not be. A sinner's blindness never suspects the real desert of sin:—much less can it imagine a blood-stained ransom. There is God in that thought.

But while we thus inquire, Scripture draws back the veil, and tells us the principle, which lived in his heart. It was faith.—" By faith Abel offered unto God a more excellent sacrifice than Cain," Heb. xi. 4. Thus the case is cleared. For faith is trust in God, and humble reliance on His Word. God speaks;—and faith hears,—believes, —obeys. Faith can breathe only in the atmosphere of revelation.—It can stand only on the rock of divine promise. It has no ear, but for heavenly tidings. It can read only what the finger of God writes.—It can always give a reason, even this, "The mouth of the Lord hath spoken it."

We are sure, then, that since Abel offered in faith, he was following the positive directions of God. We are thus led to read many of the workings of his soul in this service. It cannot be, but that his parents had made known to him, in terms of shame, the enormity of their wilful fall. Hence he knew how it occurred, that he was born a child of wrath, and an heir of corrupted nature.

But could they pause here? Oh! no.—Adoring gratitude would constrain them to add, that pardon was provided, and that a Redeemer, all-qualified and mighty to save, was coming to lay down His life. They would teach, too, that a holy rite had been ordained by God to exercise faith, and to keep alive the expectation of the atoning lamb.

This was the Bible unto Abel. Here he would read the main lessons of the Gospel of salvation. He staggered not through unbelief. He embraced the truth wholly unto life eternal.—In the twilight of the world, he saw the Sun of Righteousness.

Reader, does not this bring condemnation to multitudes, who in the full blaze of light never get saving faith?

We thus gain insight into the spiritual man of Abel. He stands at this altar, a man of humility—faith—love.

He is full of self-abasement. He abhors himself in dust and ashes. His act confesses, that he is a lost, and ruined, and undone sinner. He sees, that eternal rejection is his due. He feels, that he has no power of himself to help himself.

But he is full of faith. In looking off from himself he looks upward to another. He knows, that in the heaven of heavens there lives a Saviour ready to fly down with healing in his wings. He sees in the blood of his victim, a pledge of the blood prepared to cleanse him to the very uttermost.

He is full, too, of sanctifying love. For no man can trust in mercy so full, so unmerited, so suitable, so effectual, without feeling, that thus purchased from perdition, he must live a willing sacrifice to the God of grace.

At this time there was another by the side of Abel.
But now a great gulf parts them. It was his brother Cain.
—He was born in like guilt.—He doubtless shared the
same parental instruction.—In outward advantages there
was no difference. But is their spiritual character the
same? Far otherwise. The truth, which melts the one,
only hardens the other. One receives the blessing.—The
other abides under the curse. Their dealings with God
manifest them.

It is a sad sight. But we must not shrink from observ-
ing how Cain discovers himself. He seems to come to
God.—This is good. But what does he bring?—"The
fruit of the ground." The first appearance is fair. But
the disguise falls; and we see the hideous marks, which
prove that he "was of that wicked one."

We find self-will at the root of his religion. God has
ordained the way, in which he was to be approached.
Cain thinks, that he can use a course more suited to the
majesty of heaven and the dignity of man.—He places
his puny reason above the counsels of the All-wise.—He
turns from a revealed will to grope in the darkness of his
own vain conceits.

Reader, is not this a pitiful case? But it is the delusion of many.—"Professing themselves to be wise, they
become fools."—Self-will first makes a god—then a religion—and at last a pit of destruction for itself.

We next see pride in him.—This must be, for it is the
first-born of unenlightened reason.—Creation leaves man
dust.—Sin makes him the vilest of dust. But still he
walks vaingloriously, until grace opens his eyes, and lays
him low in his proper humility. So it is with Cain. He
feels neither sin, nor need of pardon. Therefore he

proudly tramples on an offering, which tells him of nature's pollution. High-minded, he will not wash in the blood of the Redeemer, that he may be purified. Thus he is a model of that class, who, in every age, say, "We are rich and have need of nothing; and know not that they are wretched, and miserable, and poor, and blind, and naked."

There was unbelief, too. God had set before him the redemption of Jesus Christ. It was proclaimed in promise and in type. What more could have been done? But Cain believes not. Unbelief closes his eyes—he will not look to Jesus. It closes his hand—he will not lay hold on Him. It clogs his feet—he will not run to Him. It closes his ear—he will not hear of Him. It closes his mouth—he will not cry unto Him. It closes his heart—he will not receive Him.

Do you marvel at his folly? Take heed! Take heed! Conscience may know, "Thou art the man."

The end is quickly told. Bad soon becomes worse. Unbelief swiftly goes down to its place, where the Gospel is never preached, and hope never comes. God expostulates. Cain yields not. He sees the righteousness of faith, only to hate it. He seeks, by the murder of his faithful brother, to extinguish the light, which upbraids him. He falls into the recklessness of despair. And now, from his everlasting chains, he cries, Beware of rejecting the "more excellent sacrifice."

Reader, it may be, that, careful about many things, you have, hitherto, been careless concerning that which should be the main care of man. Listen, then, for a moment, I beseech you.—Do you not hear a startling question from this story? It is this. Are you a follower of Abel or of Cain? In simpler terms, are you receiving or neglecting the Lord Jesus? I say the Lord Jesus.— For this is the real point.—He was the end of the " more excellent sacrifice," which Abel brought, which Cain scorned. He is the Lamb appointed by God, accepted of God, and led to our very doors in our Bibles.

Who can utter the mighty motives, which urge the sinner to avail himself of this sacrifice? They are more than the moments of eternity. Each speaks as loud as the thunders of Sinai. Each has a thrilling clang, as the trump of God.

Only consider its real power. It is just this. It saves for ever all the souls of all poor sinners, who present it to God in faith. Now, is not your soul precious? It is so beyond all thought.—It needs redemption from wrath and ruin. Are you prepared to offer its equal price? Suppose the balances of heaven brought out.—What can you place as a counterpoise in the counter-scale? You have nothing, but what is lighter than vanity. Produce now " the more excellent sacrifice." Its worth is beyond all weight. Offer this, and you are saved. Will you now be Cain-like, and reject " the more excellent sacrifice"?

Your sins are many.—The sands of the sea-shore are few in comparison. But each must be blotted out, or you die. A sin unpardoned cannot enter heaven. What, then, will you do? One thing is clear.—You cannot undo the done. You cannot recall the past. But behold " the more excellent sacrifice." It cleanses from all sin. Through it all manner of sin is forgiven to the children of men. It makes the scarlet, white as now, and the crimson, like wool. It changes the vilest into perfect purity. Its merits can render you spotless. Will you be Cain-like, and reject " the more excellent sacrifice "?

You need peace. Satan threatens. The law condemns. Conscience accuses. Your wounds are deep. Your burdens heavy. Memory shews frightful spectres. The heart bleeds. You go mourning and heavy laden. You look to self.—It is despair. You look to the world.—It mocks your woe. You look to reform.—It is a broken cistern. You fly to outside performances of devotion.—They are reeds, which break and pierce the hand. How different is " the more excellent sacrifice! " It tells you, that God is satisfied, guilt remitted, and all accusers dumb. It thus brings peace—perfect peace, which passeth all understanding. Will you now be Cain-like, and reject " the more excellent sacrifice "?

You desire sanctification.—You pant to be conformed to the image of Christ. This is well; for it is an eternal law of God, that without holiness no man shall see His face. But holiness can be learned only at this altar. It is a sight of the dying Jesus, which kills lust. It is the shadow of the cross, which causes evil to wither. A lover of iniquity cannot dwell on this hallowed ground. But there never was a holy man, who did not live in glory in " the more excellent sacrifice." If ever you would walk with God in true righteousness, you must not be Cain-like, and reject it.

But remember this sacrifice is only one. Jesus by the one offering of Himself, once made, " hath perfected for ever them that are sanctified." Pass by it, and you can find none else. Pass by it to-day, and you may seek it in vain to-morrow. Hear, then, the voice of Abel, which calls you without delay to hasten to the one altar of salvation.

Reader, turn not from these humble lines, until in truth you can say, I rejoice in the Lord Jesus Christ, I find Him to be " the more excellent sacrifice."

THE CONSOLATION

" This same shall comfort us."—GEN. v. 29.

THUS speaks the patriarch Lamech. Such is his voice of joy, when he receives his first-born Noah. He was tilling a soil hardened by the curse—fruitful only in thorns and thistles. But now a son is given to share the painfulness of his daily toil. Cheered by this hope, he calls his name Noah, which has the meaning of Rest or Comfort.

Reader, in these simple pages there is but one thing sought: the best good of undying souls. Therefore I examine not whether this name was designed as another ray of the coming Saviour. I rather proceed to realities, which all experience. I rather turn to tidings, which are bright on the Gospel surface.

I first state a fact, which is ancient as the fall, and wide-spread as man. It is this—A sinful world is a tearful world. Wherever we stand, our shadow is sorrow. It was so before the flood. It is so now. In all climes and ranks, the head is weary, and the heart is sick.

I next state a truth, which came in, as twin-born, with the earliest promise. It is this—Consolation is provided. God has sent forth Christ Jesus from the bosom of His love to be the Consolation of this woe-worn world.

It is my longing desire that this heavenly knowledge should more largely shed its pure balm. I mourn, that

men should drink nothing but the dregs of bitterness,
while healing streams flow fast beside them.   Let me
invite you, then, to come with me for a few moments
into some of the chambers of earth's grief.   I can show
you there, the Spirit helping, that in Jesus Christ there
is a pillow for the throbbing brow—a cordial for the
fainting spirit—a plank for the sinking—a haven for the
tempest-tossed.

I need scarcely say, that the heart of misery is misery
of heart;—the soul of anguish is anguish of soul.   But
where is the home of this extreme distress? Surely in the
breast of him, whose conscience is awake to discern the
nature—the evil—the wages—of his sins.   The nest of
self-delusion has now become a bed of thorns.   Before his
eyes God frowns, terrible in justice.   In his ears the law
thunders a tremendous curse.   He moves forward, and
there is a gaping hell.   Shall he stir—the next step may
cast him headlong into flames.   Shall he sleep—he may
awake among the lost.

Whence can comfort reach a mind thus tortured?   It
cannot spring from earth.   For let the world now present
its every charm; how worthless are they! The world has
nothing, but for a sin-blinded man.   When things are
seen as they really are, earthly toys are worse than empty
bubbles.   Comfort, to be comfort now, must come from
heaven.   All is mockery, except it can tell of God reconciled—sin pardoned—the soul safe.   Now Jesus can raise
out of these lowest depths; and He alone.—He can guide
the trembler to His cross.—He can reveal to him there
a heavenly Father, arrayed in glories of eternal love.—
He can point to His own dying as the death of wrath.
—He can show the sword of justice sheathed in His own

heart—the flames of vengeance quenched in His own blood—the hand, that was uplifted to strike, now extended to bless—all hell piled upon the Guiltless, and heaven freely given to the guilty.

Is not this Consolation? It is;—and Jesus pours it from His wounded hands and pierced side. Is not this, I repeat, Consolation? Ask those who have tasted it. Ask the jailor. Terror-stricken he sprang in—wrath was at his heels—he heard of Jesus—peace soothed his fears, and he rejoiced, believing in God with all his house, Acts xvi, 29, 31.

But it occurs, alas! too often, that they, who have escaped, as drowning mariners, to this rock, are enticed again to stray. They cease to watch and pray. Then the tempter finds an open door. They neglect the preserving means of grace. Then the foe creeps in. The Spirit is grieved and withdraws. Corruptions regain their power. Woe to backsliders! what wretchedness is theirs! Consciousness of peril returns, and it is embittered by keen self-reproach. They see how basely they have deserted the Friend, who had said to them, while in their blood, Live.

Reader, perhaps this agony is yours. You once had rest in Jesus, but it is gone. The fault is wholly your own. He did not drive you from Him. You would depart. And now you sigh, Oh! that it were with me, as in the days when the Sun of Righteousness shone upon my path. Be not tearless, for grievous is your fall. But be not hopeless, for Jesus is yet near. His voice still follows you, " Return, and I will not cause mine anger to fall upon you," Jer. iii. 12. In nothing is His tenderness more tender, than in stilling the sobs of those who sob in penitence before Him. Return then. The Lord still extends the arms of His pitifulness. He is the balm in Gilead. He is the Physician there. He cannot be silent to the cry, "Restore to me the joy of Thy salvation."

There are others, who closely cling to the Lord, and yet are disquieted. They gratefully acknowledge, "Hitherto hath the Lord helped us;" but heaven seems far off; the pilgrimage is long; adversaries are many; their own strength totters;—they look to the winds and waves, and trembling takes hold upon them; they say with David, we shall one day perish by the hand of Saul.

Reader, perhaps you have such heart-felt misgivings. Truly if Jesus were other than He is, you might thus faint. But now I am bold to bid you arise and shake yourself from the dust. Open your eyes and read His heart.—It speaks one language. It is all encouragement. It tells of faithful love, which, as it never had beginning, so it can have no end. He draws you to the shelter of His wings, and there stifles each rising doubt by assurances as large as they are free;—as gentle as they are countless. He tells you, "Because I live, ye shall live also." "Your life is hid with Christ in God." If you ask richer Consolation, you ask more than God can give.

But afflictions break upon you with ceaseless tide. This is to be expected. It is our common lot. There is no home so lowly, but some sorrow finds the door. There is no palace so upraised, but some sorrow mounts the steps. Faith shields not from this. "In the world ye shall have tribulation." But welcome all sorrow, if Jesus enters by its side! This always is so to the true believer.

Health may wither like a fading flower; languor and

disease may feed upon the frame; there may be tossings to and fro until the dawning of the day. But Jesus can relax with smiles the pain-contracted brow, and beguile with songs the wakeful night.

Earthly possessions may crumble to decay; poverty may sit where affluence was wont to smile. But can the believer's portion fail? Oh! no: he has all the treasures in the word, "The Lord is my Shepherd, I shall not want."

Friends may forsake; averted looks may chill. There may be treachery or open hate, where once much love was feigned. Jesus knew this trial in its bitterest form. Hence He is quick to prove that He changes not with the changing world. He magnifies His sympathy by sticking closer than a brother, His own presence more than fills each void within.

But death draws on with rapid step. Yes: it will soon draw back the covers of your bed, and extend an icy hand to bear you hence. You will then need strong Consolation. Long-tried props can prop no more. Alone you must go through the dark valley. But not alone?— For Jesus whispers, "I am with you. Thus I guide to my many-mansioned home." So the last trial is the last and largest Consolation.

Believer, let me pray you to live and die leaning on Jesus as your Consolation. Would you be expert in this happy art? Make it, then, your daily habit to meditate upon Himself—His promises—His dealings. Hold close communion with Him. Measure the breadth, the length, the depth, the height of His office and His work. Be assured, that all that He is, and all that He has, and all that He has done, and all that He is doing, and all that He will do, is yours.—You have never been absent from His heart, and never can be. You are a member " of His body, of His flesh, and of His bones."—Abide in Him at all seasons, and all seasons will be comfort.

Strike, too, the rock of the promises with the rod of faith. Sweet waters will gush out. They will flow very deep, and very broad, and all within this channel, " Comfort ye, comfort ye, my people, saith your God."

Take frequent walks also by the side of the faithful pilgrims of old. Precious is their companionship. They may be sorrowful, yet they are always rejoicing. They may be homeless wanderers, as Jacob was, yet they are comforted. They may pine long in dungeons and under evil fame, as Joseph did, yet they are comforted. They may be destitute of all things, as Elijah was, yet they are comforted. They may flee for their lives and hide themselves in caves of the earth, as David did, yet they are comforted. They may be in the hottest fire of persecution, as the three captive youths were, yet they are comforted. They may be in all perils, and in the wildest storms, as Paul was; they may be called to bear faithful witness in scoffing crowds, or before frowning tyrants, as this apostle was, yet they are comforted. They may die the martyr's death under showers of crushing stones, as Stephen did, yet they are comforted. They may lose all things, yet they never lose the Consolation, which is in Christ Jesus. It is the work of His Spirit.—It is the gift of His grace.—It is the token of His indwelling.— It is the foretaste of His heaven.

Perhaps the eyes of some rest upon these pages, who are strangers to this deep well-spring of Consolation. Unhappy men! Your hearts are a disconsolate blank.

You have been sowing vanity, and what do you now reap? You have made the world your all, what has it given you? If much be obtained, more is coveted. Possession contents not. Pursuit wearies. This hour is fretfulness. The next is a dreaded abyss. You wander over fields of anxiety, and there is no seat of rest. Society is a hollow insipidity. Solitude is a dismal gloom. Where are your comforts? There are none in the retrospect, none in hand, none in the horizon. The past upbraids, the present dissatisfies, the future terrifies.

A condemning voice within tells you, that is true. Turn not, then, from the beseeching voice of this page. —Be persuaded. Consent, consent to be happy.—" Seek ye the Lord, while He may be found." " Take with you words." Plead with Him His office, " The Lord hath anointed Me to comfort all that mourn in Zion."—Plead with Him His call, " Come unto Me, all ye that are weary and heavy laden, and I will give you rest."—Plead with Him His promise, " I will not leave you comfortless."—Plead with Him His title, " The Consolation of Israel."—Plead with Him His tender voice, " As one, whom his mother comforteth, so will I comfort you."— Plead with Him the awful gulf between the saved and the lost, " Now he is comforted, and thou art tormented." —Plead with him the command from heaven, " Comfort ye, comfort ye my people, saith your God."—Cease not thus to plead, until you can say of Him, who is far greater than Noah, " This same shall comfort us."

THE ARK

*"The Lord said unto Noah, Come thou and all thy
house into the ark."*—GEN. vii. 1.

THE story of the ark has been familiar to us from
memory's birth. It gave interest to our earliest
lessons. Its very name revives the instructions by a
tender mother's side, or from some anxious teacher's lips.
It brings us back to the first pages of our first Bible, and
to our seats as children in our childhood's class.

In a land of Christian teaching, most in their youth
thus pondered the record of a wretched world's most
wretched end. In thought they trace and retrace each
particular, until the whole is vivid, as a witnessed scene.
But they, who go no deeper, only trifle as with a nursery-
toy. Their feet reach the threshold of truth's palace, but
they enter not into the wide chamber, in which God dis-
penses light. They break not the box of precious ointment. They are like Hagar. A well of water is near.—
She thirsts, but sees it not.

Reader, be not deceived. The Bible is a mirror in
your hands for this grand end,—that you may see therein
a loving Saviour's loving heart, and a mighty Saviour's
mighty deeds. He is the treasure of the field of Scripture.
If you win Him, you are rich and wise for ever. If you
win Him not, all other wealth is penury: all other
knowledge is a brilliant folly. Act on this soul-saving

principle; and never close the sacred pages, until you are cheered by the smile of Him, who is the smile of heaven.

Come, then, and with holy longing after the light of life, let us contemplate the Ark. Jesus is there in all the glories of redeeming love.

"Make thee an ark of gopher wood."—Here is no human forethought. It is a voice from heaven. But for what purpose? The reply pencils the dark back-ground, on which the bright features of God's grace appear most prominent in beauty.

"God saw that the wickedness of man was great in the earth, and that every imagination of the thoughts of his heart was only evil continually," or every day. Sin enormous—sin all-prevailing—sin without ceasing, was the vapour which went up from earth.

But can sin thus rear its head, and wrath lie still? Impossible! Sin is the abominable thing, which God hates. It cannot move onward without dragging vengeance in the rear.

Behold the proof. God the holy and the just proclaims, "The end of all flesh is come before me." But would any plead that the threat was vague, and gave no definite alarm? Judgment draws not the glittering sword, until the clearest trumpets sound the clearest sound. Mark the next thrilling note, "Behold I, even I, do bring a flood of waters upon the earth." Thus all might know what terrors were gathering around. Thus all heard the tolling of execution's bell.

God is righteous. He strikes not without cause.—He strikes not without warning.—The notice, though thus distinct, seems to have been uttered only by one preacher's voice. But who can count the messages upon messages, throughout all ages, which have clustered around our earth, each testifying, that the day of judgment and perdition of ungodly men draweth nigh?

Reader, you have been often told, that everlasting burnings are the bed of sin.

The threatened vengeance moved with reluctant step. Longsuffering suffered long. Years dawned and closed, and still the sun was bright, the skies were clear. Surely if space for repentance brought the grace of repentance, the world would have been clad in sackcloth of penitence and shame. But something far mightier than external opportunity must work, before a soul can feel, and confess, and forsake its sins. Man, not arrested from on high, is man going downward in guilt. A lengthened respite is often nothing but a lengthened iniquity.

I pray you, apply this. It is not mine to know your years, your warnings, or your calls. But years you have; and warnings you have had; and every moment is a call. Say, then, has the goodness of God led you to repentance? Let conscience answer. Believe me, reprieves are not pardons. Execution delayed is not execution escaped. Agag is spared to-day, to die more signally to-morrow. If you are still a wanderer from God, let this hour see your tears, and hear your prayers; or soon you may never cease to weep, where prayer is never made.

Amidst this spreading flood of evil the ark continues to rise. Noah had heard the word, " Make thee an Ark." The command was startling. He was to provide against a judgment, new and unknown. Reason would question, how can it be? Experience,—which knew not the like,—would darken doubts. Prejudice, with many ready cavils, would hint that it was improbable, if not impossible. But God hath spoken—The man of God was persuaded.—He acted, and prepared, and was saved.

It could scarcely be, but that ridicule and sneer would embitter his days of trustful toil. Many, who marked, would mock his unabating labour.—He would stand a very by-word for brain-sick delusion. This is faith's constant trial.—The natural man understands not its motives, its hopes, its expectations, its doings.—But it is quick of ear to hear, and quick of eye to see a guiding God. It well knows whom it believes. It has an assurance far more assured than all conclusions of reason or testimonies of sense. Thus nothing moves it. It tramples down hindrances. It embraces the cross, and wins the crown.

The last hour strikes at last. The cup of iniquity overflows. Who now can stay the right hand of the Lord?— The clouds gather,—the ceaseless torrents fall. Where now is the jest,—the taunt,—the bravery of unbelief? The truth of God is a truth discovered too late. Destruction is found to be a reality, when the victim feels the grasp. Refuge has ceased. The loftiest buildings, the tops of the highest rocks, are only a watery grave. Earth is a whirlpool of despair, and then the silence of departed life.

Such is the solemn fact. Wrath denounced, and wrath not feared, is wrath without escape. But hearken! for every drop of this huge deluge has a voice, which sighs; as surely as the ungodly of the old world once lived, so surely did they sink in anguish. The word of God responds with as many tongues; as surely as men tread the same earth, so surely will the final flames burst forth.

What! though the hour be not expected.—Unheeded slumber is one sign that it is near. Decreasing moments will soon decrease no more. A worn out thread scarcely restrains the sluices of a fiery flood. The end rolls forward.—Soon, and it will be here.—Soon, and it will be past.—Soon, and we shall have had our part in it.

Reader, will it find you in the Ark of salvation, or writhing in the billows of the lost? Pause, and reflect. The world decrepit and blind in sin, is tottering to the gulf of ruin. Are you, then, secure in an all-sufficient haven; or are you unsheltered, as a tiny bark in the midst of a wild ocean's roar?

Why do I thus ask? Because I would have you safe, and happy, and peaceful, and blessed for ever. But safety there is none: —happiness there is none: —peace there is none: —and blessedness there is none, except in the Gospel-ark, which is Christ Jesus.

Behold Him! Behold Him! What is the Ark of old to us, but an emblem of His full redemption? He is the one deliverance from all peril. He is the heaven-high refuge. He is the all-protecting safety. He is the building of enduring life; the foundation of which was laid in the counsels of eternity; which was reared in the fulness of time on the plains of earth; and the head of which towers above the skies. He is that lofty fabric of shelter, which God decreed, appointed, provided, and sets before the sons of men. He is that sure covert, which is so fortified, that all the thunderbolts of the almightiness of divine judgment play harmless around it; and all the raging storms of vengeance, and all the fury of the waves of wrath, only consolidate its strength. It must be so.

For our hiding place is the mighty God. Our salvation is Jehovah's fellow. Our glorious sanctuary is the glorious Jesus.

This Ark is brought very near—even to your feet. Its portals are widely open. All things call you, nay, command you to come in. God's finger writes above the door, whosoever enters is for ever safe. No powers of earth or hell can injure or affright the rescued inmates.

Do you pause? Alas! too many a brow proclaims in letters of worldly-mindedness, frivolity, indifference, profaneness, sin,—"as our fathers were, so are we." But will you be self-slain? Would that I could pierce the windings of your heart, and detect the fatal hesitation, which administers its opiate there! I would drag the monster into light.—I would give you no rest, until you had trampled it to death.

Think, do any of the following marks betray the foes, which lodge, as murderers within you.

Convictions are sometimes hushed by the silly smile, we are only as the mass around us. If we are in peril, who is not? Can these crowds all perish? Surely there is mercy in God, which will hold back such an ocean of unfathomable woe. This thought is an old deceiver. Numbers change not the truth of God, or the character of sin; neither can they frame a bark to float on waves of fire.

Youth, if it think at all, may think, that coming years will bring some refuge.—This is an idle dream. When did hardened hardness melt into softness? Will unbelief, by growing old, ripen into faith? The morning of life was no barrier against the flood. Who can count the cradles which it devoured? If you are young, be wise, and laugh not through a speck of time, and then wail through an immeasurable eternity.

Others are at ease, because they have been taught the truths of Jesus. The Ark was well studied of old. Day after day it was the gaze and discourse of thousands. But this saved not. They who trust to the mere acquaintance of the mind, will find their memory a keen edge to the gnawings of the undying worm.

It may be, that in forms, and ordinances, and services, you draw very near, and seem to place your hands on saving grace. Thus many touched the Ark, and did no more. As the water rose, they would cling to it with agonized grasp. In vain.—They are without.—And all without is death.

Others hope, ere it be too late, to cry and pray. How many sank in fruitless shriekings for some help!

Perchance you are high in gifts, in talents, in position, in influence, in diligence, in self-esteem, in man's applause. But as the peaks, which soared above the clouds, dwindled before the flood; so the loftiest pretensions are very dust before the great white throne.

Is it so, that you have a shadowy hope, that at last something self-framed, will be a plank of escape? Many devices were devised, when the deluge began its unsparing work. But all were as a mocking straw.

Reader, be not cheated of your soul's life-blood by impostors in such thin disguise. Turn to the truth of God. Seek the one real, solid, substantial provision, to which our Bibles point with extended arm. There is but one name under heaven given among men, whereby we must be saved. There is but one security. We are safe only, when enclosed and wrapped up in Christ. We are above peril only, when dwelling within Him, the Ark. We are covered only, when we nestle in His wounded side. We are hid only, when gathered under His wide-spread wings.

Never rest till you have passed the threshold of this heaven-wrought Ark. Then you may rejoice with the people of God. " Surely in the floods of great waters they shall not come nigh unto him," Ps. xxxii. 6.

THE ALTAR

"Noah builded an altar unto the Lord."—GEN. viii. 20.

TO know the sanctifying power of grace, we must trace its actings in holy men. A machine of many wheels is a complex puzzle, until each part is seen in motion and in work. Thus it is by close study of godly models, that we learn what spiritual temples can arise from vile materials of earth; and how poor sinners, weak as we are, can quit themselves like heroes in the field of trial.

The scene may vary with the sun and with the cloud. But still some prominent marks can never be obscured. The child of God will always exhibit ready obedience to a heavenly Father's will—undoubting trust in His Word—calm submission to His guidance—constant approach to Him through reconciling blood,—and hallowed joy in prayer and praise. It is no tree of faith, if it be not laden with these fruits. It is no purified metal if it be not stamped with this image. It is no heaven-born soul unless it prove its descent by these features. It is no heavenward walk, except along this consecrated road.

The truth of this is written, as with a sunbeam, in the annals of Noah. God said, " Make thee an ark." The work, though strange, is instantly begun. The Lord calls, " Come thou and all thy house into the ark." If there be perils without, there are also countless perils within. But in calm confidence he enters;—and in following the Lord fully, he has all safety and all peace. Again the same voice speaks, "Go forth of the ark." He leaves his refuge to stand on the grave of a buried world. He had known the earth as the riot-house of evil; but now it is a noiseless solitude. He reads in one vast ruin the epitaph of sin.

It is rightly concluded, that worship was his first employ. "Noah builded an altar unto the Lord." The peculiar moment gives peculiar complexion to this act. Matters upon matters were crowding for attention. He was houseless.—There was no fold for the herds.—He had all to do; and all demanded thought, and plan, and arrangement, and effort, and toil. If ever man might plead that distracting necessities excluded God, Noah was that man. If ever there was a time too full for thoughts of heaven, this was the time. But no. All shall yield to Him, who is above all. He, who is First, shall have the first. He, who is Best, shall have the best. The earth's first building is an Altar to its Maker. The patriarch's first care is to bless the care, which has so cared for him. His first posture is the bended knee and the uplifted hand.

If I seem to linger on the outskirts of my subject, it is to press this point: Satan often holds back the arm upraised to knock at mercy's gate by the check, Not now,—not yet. Earthly duties must have their dues. This hour is claimed by the family—the trade—or rest. Listen not. No time is lost by giving it to God. No work is good, except begun, continued, and ended in Him. Devote to Him your earliest—your last. He will not be your debtor. He, who never can be paid, will more than overpay you.

The Altar was raised, that offerings might bleed thereon. You doubt not, that the dying victim and the flowing blood pictured the dying of the Lamb of God. This is the first letter of the Gospel-primer. It is, however, equally true, though not so obvious, that the Altar preaches Him, who is the sum and substance of redemption's wonders. Jesus is every part of sin's atonement. As He is the true Priest, and the true slain one, so, too, He is the true Altar. He presents Himself to die upon Himself.

Believer, thus your sacrifice is perfect because it is entirely divine. You have a Priest,—and only one; and He is passed into the heavens, and sits at the right hand of the Majesty on high. You have a Lamb—and only one. No more is needed. And He died but once; for once was absolutely sufficient to satisfy and save. So, too, you have an Altar, and only one. It ever stands before the throne of God. Jesus is this Altar.

This is no dream of fancy. It is the faithful saying of our God. The Spirit Himself leads to the Altar, and bids us read in it this Gospel-lesson. He guided the Apostle's lips to utter, "We have an Altar," Heb. xiii. 10. Therefore an Altar is counted among our treasures. But where is it? It must be where the Priest is, and where the blood is. They are not here. They are within the veil of heaven. There, too, is our Altar; and, being in heaven, it can only be the Lord Jesus. This is the well of truth, which the Spirit opens. With joy let us draw water from it.

The Altar has many uses; but this is the main;—it is

the victim's dying bed. Hence Jesus, when He comes to die, must have such bed. Now, let faith go back to Calvary,—the cradle of its hopes. There, in the fulness of time, our great High Priest is seen, leading a willing Lamb. The Lamb is Himself. It bears no common burden, "for the Lord hath laid on Him the iniquities of us all." The weight of one sin would thrust a soul for ever and ever, downward and downward, deeper and deeper into the bottomless pit of woe. But who can count the sins under which Jesus groans? The number is infinite, and each a mass which knows no measure.

On what altar, then, can this heavy-laden sufferer lie? Let all angels spread beneath Him their combined strength—it is but a broken reed. Shall worlds be piled upon worlds?—They would crumble into dust. Heaven can give no aid. It is all dark above, when Jesus cries, " My God, My God, why hast Thou forsaken me?" Earth has fled. He looked, but there was no man.

But all that He needed, He was in Himself. His Deity is the Altar of His expiring humanity. He is His own succour. Supported by Himself, He fails not under the whole flood of Jehovah's outpoured wrath. Upheld by Himself, He drinks the last dreg of the cup of fury. Firm on this rock, He pays, until justice cries, Enough. Strong in His own might, He satisfies, until satisfaction overflows. Immovably based on His own Godhead, He blots out iniquity, until iniquity no more is found.

Reader, I thus earnestly exalt Jesus, as the one Altar of expiation, that you may learn more clearly, that He is All in buying the soul from death. Believe me, it is not easy, it is not common, to see this truth in its unclouded glory. Satan and all hell strain every nerve at every moment to darken it with mists. Poor nature is prone to drink the potion, that some help from Christ makes all things safe. Self, bewitched with self, and self-performances, fondles the conceit, that man's meritoriousness, decked with Christ's merits, is the key of heaven. What is this, but to build an altar of human rubbish, with human tools, and then add Christ thereto?

This is the delusion, which, with Christ on its front, stalks through the earth, and murders thousands. This is the poison tree, beneath the shade of which, many lie down and dream that they make Christ their only hope, while the main weight of trust is hung on self. This is the fiend, which mocks the lost, by showing them too late that Christ extolled in name, is not Christ reigning in the heart. This is the foe, which often makes the faithful ministry a fruitless field. Men fancy that to hear of Christ, and to commend the sound, amounts to saving grace.—Self, in some form, is earth's loved altar.

Here is the deep mischief of the Church of Rome. Here is the net so speciously wrought—so craftily spread —by that power of darkness. That heresy admits enough of Christ to calm the conscience, but it retains enough of self to slay the soul. It denies not, that Jesus lived and died to save: but it denies that Jesus alone can suffice. It therefore erects altars very many—and very high—and very captivating to sense and fancy. It makes these the real groundwork of the sinner's hope. It then surmounts the whole with Christ, and, like a Babel-builder, thinks that the summit will extend to heaven. There is a semblance of uplifting Christ. But it is Christ added to angels—Christ added to saints—Christ added to a train of mediators and intercessors—Christ added to the church—Christ added to penance—Christ added to purgatory—Christ, as the pinnacle of a pyramid of man's deserts.

This is the papal Gospel. But the feet of the image are of clay. It cannot stand;—and its downfall will crush, like Dagon's temple.

Others sport with this idol, who are papists in heart, though not in name. They find an altar in forms, and services, and self-denials, and superstitions. They build on a foundation of their own, and then call Christ to decorate their structure. They grant, that the scale is light without Him; so at last they cast in the plea of His merits to supply defects. This creed may seem to lead to life, but it goes down to hell. The word is sure, "Christ is become of no effect unto you, whosoever of you are justified by the law; ye are fallen from grace," Gal. v. 4.

But there are other uses of the altar. It received the gifts and first fruits of the worshipper. From it supplies of food were taken. To it the guilty fled. Its ground was a sanctuary; its horns a refuge. Jesus is all this.

Reader, your calling is to dedicate yourself—your soul —your body—all that you are—all that you have—all that you can do—a sacrifice to God. You may not keep anything from Him, who has given more than all heaven for your ransom. Settle this truth, then, steadily in your mind; that there is no acceptance for person, or services, except in the Beloved. Words and works are worse than worthless, except when offered in the faith, and through the merits, and for the sake of Jesus. That fruit is only rotteness, which is not sanctified by His blood, and consecrated to His glory. Cement yourself,—your every intent,—your every doing to Him. Nothing but the rich incense, which curls from this Altar, can render you, and your life, a sweet savour unto God.

Reader, be much in prayer. This is the breath of a living soul. Each moment is a need, each moment should be a heaven-ascending cry. But it is only at one altar, that petitions gain power to prevail. Supplicants, with Christ in their arms, take heaven by storm. But prayer unmixed with Christ, is a smoke vanishing into air. It is scattered, as the chaff of the summer threshing-floors.

Abound, too, in thanksgiving. The command is, " In everything give thanks." The tide of mercies ever flows. Shall the stream of grateful love ever ebb? But it is no welcome praise, unless it be fragrant from this Altar. Adoration must here plume its wings, or it can never fly above the skies.

The soul needs hourly food. And it is here that it must seek refreshment. Rich indeed is the repast to which the Gospel calls! The word—the promises—the ordinances—the sacraments—are spread as an abundant feast. But it is Christ, who constitutes the essence of the nourishment. Apart from Him means of grace are but a choking husk.

The Altar, too, had horns. The offender clinging to them was safe. No avenging hand could touch him. Thus all, who flee to Christ, may smile at every foe. No threat of the law, no sword of justice, no pursuer's rage can harm.

Happy the believer, who has made this Altar the home of his safe delights! Beneath its shelter he will often resolve, Here I have laid down the burden of my every sin; here will I add, by the Spirit's power, the whole of a devoted and adoring life. He, who is the Altar on which I die to sin, shall be the Altar on which I live to God. For pardon and for godliness, Christ shall be my All.

THE SWEET SAVOUR

" The Lord smelled a sweet savour."—GEN. viii. 21.

READER, do not you desire that your soul may prosper at the throne of grace? Perhaps you reply, Such blessedness is beyond all price. But how can one so mean as a creature,—so vile as a sinner, gain happy acceptance?

Blessed be God! there is a ready door. Draw near, leaning by faith on the arm of Jesus,—robed by faith in His righteousness,—pleading by faith the costly merits of His blood, and you enter encircled with songs of welcome. All heaven rejoices over you with joy unutterable.

Our Bible seems written with the grand intent thus to guide, by an everliving way, to the rest of God. Therefore it is, that in its pages we see the golden portals flying open, when touched by hands like ours. Abel comes with the appointed Lamb;—no frown repels him. " God had respect unto Abel, and to his offering." Noah comes with the same key;—no bolts obstruct him. His service is grateful incense. " The Lord smelled a sweet savour."

So it ever has been. So it ever must be. There is a virtue in the death of Jesus, so precious, so mighty, that it has resistless power with God. Whenever the poor sinner presents it, there is new chorus to the hymns on high; " again they say Hallelujah."

How important is it, that this truth should be as a sun

without a speck before us! Hence the Spirit records, that when Noah shed the blood which represented Christ, "The Lord smelled a sweet savour." Thus the curtains of God's pavilion are thrown back; and each attribute appears rejoicing in redemption. The Lamb is offered, and there is fragrance throughout heaven.

O my soul, these are blessed tidings. They show the irresistible plea, by which we may obtain pardon, and every needful grace. This lesson might indeed have been spread over a wide expanse of reasoning and of proof; and still the outline might have been scarcely touched. But the Spirit simply states, "The Lord smelled a sweet savour." We catch one glance, and all is seen. The cross is raised, and clouds of prevailing odour pierce the skies.

This image is a bright jewel in the Bible-treasury, because it speaks the language of every class, in every age, in every clime. It was light to pious pilgrims in patriarchal times. After the lapse of centuries, it is equally light to us. It revived our elder brethren. It will revive the latest saint. It stoops to the lowliness of the most lowly hut. It soars above the loftiness of the most lofty intellect. "The Lord smelled a sweet savour." All read and understand alike, that Jehovah reposes in Jesus, and is satisfied to the extent of Deity.

Just as one orb contains all light, so this brief word is the whole Gospel of reconciliation. The children of Israel were taught in the twilight-rites the fulness of the work of Christ. The flowing blood preached all forgiveness. But to assure their hearts, over each victim this olive-branch was waved;—"The priest shall burn all on the altar to be a burnt-sacrifice, an offering made by fire, of a sweet savour unto the Lord," Lev. i. 9.

So, too, when the Apostle uplifts the cross, he proves its power by the same emblem. "Christ also hath loved us, and hath given Himself for us, an offering and a sacrifice to God for a sweet smelling savour," Eph. v. 2. This is the magnifying medium, through which we see, that the dying of Jesus is the garden of God's sweetest perfumes. His one sacrifice is eternal and unbounded fragrance.

Let us now draw nearer, and learn how the whole Godhead here expands itself in limitless delights. When we contemplate God in His majesty, we see upon His head the many crowns of every pure and holy excellence. They all shine in one grand harmony of infinite, unchangeable glory. They cannot be parted. They cannot exist asunder. They are united by bands, which God alone could frame, but which God can never disunite. The question instantly arises, How can they all concur in raising a sinner to share the Eternal's throne?

First, let Justice speak. Its claim strikes terror. It has a right to one unbroken series of uninterrupted obedience through all life's term. Each straying of a thought from perfect love incurs a countless debt. It has in its hand an immeasurable roll, written within and without against us. If it be willing to relax, it connives at evil,— and God ceases to be God. Therefore it sternly cries, pay me what thou owest. But how shall he pay, who has nothing of his own but sin?—Behold the Cross. Here Jesus pays down a death, the worth of which no tongue can reckon. Justice hold scales, which groan indeed under mountains upon mountains of iniquity: but this one sacrifice more than outweighs the pile. Thus Justice rejoices, because it is infinitely honoured. For if all the family of man had been cast into the prison-house of torment: —if they had writhed for ever, paying the penalty of hell-pains: —the whole could never have been cancelled. Eternity could not have seen the end. But Jesus dies, and Justice at once is crowned with everlasting satisfaction.

A case from common life, though far short of the entire truth, may help to clear it to our view. A debtor's debt amounts to thousands. His means can render a penny on each day. The creditor arrests him and takes the daily mite. Years pass, but the mass scarcely lessens. The removal of a daily grain will not wear out the ocean's sands. But let a rich man come, and in one sum discharge the whole. The claim ceases. The prisoner goes free. The creditor exults in a payment, which is unlooked-for gain. Thus at the cross, Justice receives a cup of atonement, so full, that it can hold no more. It revels in the sweetness of the savour.

Ponder the wonders which are here achieved. Justice not only drops its avenging sword, but it becomes arrayed in smiles of approving love. It is no more an adversary, —demanding condemnation. It stands, as an advocate, insisting on acquittal. The principle, which rigidly requires death for each sin, as rigidly refuses to take the payment twice. Cling then to the cross. There Justice, by a mighty plea, establishes your right to heaven.

Next, there is a sweet savour here to the Truth of God. If Justice is unyielding, so too, is Truth. Its yea is yea; its nay is nay. It speaks, and the word must be. Heaven and earth may pass away, but it cannot recede. Now its voice is gone forth, denouncing eternal wrath on every sin. Thus it bars heaven's gates with bars of adamant. In vain are tears, and penitence, and prayers. Truth be-

comes untrue, if sin escapes. But Jesus comes to drink the
cup of vengeance. Every threat falls on His Head. Truth
needs no more. It claps the wings of rapturous delight,
and speeds to heaven to tell that not one word has failed.

Take another faint image. A king issues a decree.
His oath is pledged that death shall follow disobedience.
A subject rebels. He is convicted. Execution is required.
If the king hesitate, where is his faithfulness, and where
is the majesty of his empire? But let the king's son, in
the offender's stead, endure the penalty. Then the law
is magnified, the statute is inviolate, the sacredness of
order rejoices, while the guilty lives. Thus, when Jesus
suffers, Truth gains honour for its every saying, and
smells a sweet savour of content.

Believer, rejoice in the cross. Here the Word, which
had forged such mighty chains, finds that it can only live
in your life. It demands salvation for you; for it has
nothing against you, but all for you in the unalterable
promise, " Whosoever believeth in Him shall not perish,
but have everlasting life."

Need I add, that Jesus is a sweet savour to the Holiness
of God. This perfection is the sensitive plant of heaven.
It recoils from the approach of sin. It cannot look upon
uncleanness. It has no eye, but for unsullied righteousness. It only breathes where all is pure. Now, at the
cross a marvel is effected, which is joy to every fibre of
its heart, A stream thence flows, which washes out the
crimson-dye, until it can be no more found. Nor is this
all. The sinner looks to it, and, as he gazes, the love of
evil withers, and the love of God buds forth. Thus the
cross presents to Holiness " a glorious Church, not having
spot, or wrinkle, or any such thing."

Reader, would you obtain a title and fitness for heaven? Live at the cross. It gives a meetness to inherit. It gives an aptness to enjoy.

Ministers of Christ, would you weaken the sway of Satan? Preach the cross. They only die to the rule of sin, who die in Jesus to its penalties. There is no sanctifying principle but faith in Christ.

Sweet too is the savour which mercy here inhales. Mercy weeps over misery. In all afflictions it is afflicted. It tastes the bitterest drop in each cup of woe. But when anguish is averted, the guilty spared, the perishing rescued, and all tears wiped from the eyes of the redeemed, then is its holiest triumph. Loud is its rapture, when it sees a countless multitude snatched from the bitterest agonies; and borne to celestial bliss. Overflowing is its delight, when it hears voices, like ocean's waters, hymning the victories of the Lamb. Infinite is its joy, when it realizes, that this adoration will swell louder in melody through endless ages. But it is only at the cross, that Mercy raises this exulting head.

I am painfully aware, that many of the sons of sin have some vague thought of finding mercy without finding Christ. Oh! that they might learn, ere it be too late, that God's mercy never moves from Calvary.

Reader, I trust, that you now distinctly see, how every attribute sings, and rejoices, and gives thanks, and glories in the all-satisfying Jesus. His incense ascends, and heaven luxuriates in the savour. Hence the Father brings in the Son with the happy voice, "Behold mine elect, in whom my soul delighteth;" and again, "This is my beloved Son, in whom I am well pleased."

Reader, is the like mind in you? Is the joy of heaven

your joy? Is its refreshment the refreshment of your heart? Is its perfume the perfume of your spirit? Does your every faculty expand and recreate in Jesus? Is He your Paradise of every spice and every flower? Is He your Garden of Eden, in which each moment is a moment of blossoming, and each blossom opens in increasing fragrance?

Believe me, every sweet savour is in Him. Believe me, there is no sweet savour elsewhere. The world is a foul desert. The vapour of its weeds is corruption and rottenness. Turn from its thorns and briers. Come and walk up and down in the verdant places of the Gospel. Partake of the deliciousness which here abounds. The ransomed all sing in the ways of the Lord; " His name is as ointment poured forth: " " He is the Rose of Sharon: " " A bundle of myrrh is my Beloved unto me: " " He is as a cluster of camphire: " " All thy garments smell of myrrh, and aloes, and cassia: " He is the sweet savour, which can never fail.

Can any hear this and turn to Christless habits? Ah! child of sin, pause, I beseech you. Apart from Christ, your person is accursed—Your merit is a filthy rag—Your prayer is an abomination—Your praise is an insult— Your service is a mockery—Your walk is a daily step from God—Your death is a downfall into hell. Tell me, is it not far better to be unto God a sweet savour of Christ? Think! a life redolent of Christ will be an eternity of fragrance through the realms of light. But a life, which is the scent of earth's corruptions, becomes at last a loathsome fume in the charnel-house of darkness.

THE BOW IN THE CLOUD

" I do set my Bow in the Cloud."—GEN. ix. 13.

IN the rainbow there is a charm, of which every eye is conscious. It looks forth through the dark windows of the storm, and earth rejoices in the reviving visit. Its lovely hues proclaim that the gloom is past. It spans the clouds, as the fair herald of returning clearness. Its noble form, its various shades of distinct and blended colour, surpass all praise. Admiration can only say, It worthily magnifies its mighty Maker.

Such delights become us. The book of nature is the penmanship of God. Every line should be a sanctifying lesson. Enlightened piety sings, " The works of the Lord are great, sought out of all them that have pleasure therein."

But the shining light of the Bow teaches far more than that our God is excellent to plan, and almighty to perform. To receive its especial instruction we must ponder its birth.

Let us go back, then, and take our station by the side of Noah, when it first awakened his grateful thanks.

His feet again trod on the solid pavement of earth. But the sound of rushing torrents had left their echo in his ear. The expanse of desolation had not faded from his view. What had been, might be again. Each gathering cloud might mantle the world in final ruin. Each falling drop might open the sluices of another deluge. Thus fears would lodge in his breast; and " fear hath torment."

From the foreboding patriarch, let us turn to our God. He is glorious in tenderness, and pitifulness, and compassion, and watchful care towards His people. It is His merciful will, that they should repose in perfect peace. He invites them to feed by the still waters of confiding love. He would have the wings of each breeze to flutter over them—laden with joy. He would have every shadow to spread the covert of protection.

But how will He calm the trembling anxieties of Noah? A word of heaven-sent promise might suffice. But He, who multiplies to pardon, multiplies also to give comfort. His word indeed shall go forth, but it shall go forth sealed with an enduring, ever-speaking seal. He will call a new wonder into being. A smiling offspring of the weeping cloud shall tranquilly assure the earth, that waters have no more a mandate to lay waste.

And what is this wonder? An arch, cheering and bright, embraces the firmament. On a scroll of variegated light there is inscribed, These storms drop fertility: they break to bless and not to injure.

How is this wonder framed? Jehovah's works are sublime in their simplicity. The sun looks forth from the opposite skies. Its rays enter the descending drops, and returning to the eye in broken pencils, paint the Bow on the illuminated back-ground. Heaven dries up the tears of earth, and the high roof above seems to take up the Gospel-hymn, "Glory to God in the highest, and on earth peace, good will towards men."

Thus the Bow is more than an evidence of skill and power. It is the brilliant signet on God's preserving arm. It is the golden impress, by which He ratifies the covenant, that " the waters shall no more become a flood to destroy all flesh."

But faith looks further. It is ever intent to catch the image of its beloved Lord. It has learned the sound principle, that the whole field of nature reflects the beauties and glories of Jesus. It has read the testimony, that He is the " true Light," and the " true Bread," and the " true Vine." Hence it is not slow to inquire, Is He not too the truth of the " faithful witness in Heaven?" While it thus listens to drink in some Gospel-music from the Bow, the word sounds plainly : " For a small moment have I forsaken thee : but with great mercies will I gather thee. In a little wrath, I hid My face from thee for a moment : but with everlasting kindness will I have mercy on thee, saith the Lord thy Redeemer. For this is as the waters of Noah unto Me : for as I have sworn, that the waters of Noah should no more go over the earth; so have I sworn that I would not be wroth with thee nor rebuke thee. For the mountains shall depart, and the hills be removed; but my kindness shall not depart from thee, neither shall the covenant of my peace be removed, saith the Lord that hath mercy on thee," Isaiah, liv. 7–10.

Here the great depths of God's love are broken up. As the deluge overtopped the highest hills, so this assurance drowns the pinnacles of doubt and hesitation. It places the covenant of Noah in contrast with the covenant of Jesus. God promising to hold back a flood pictures God, making oath, that He will save to the uttermost. The earth safe from watery waste is the Church safe from all wrath.

But if the former had a pledge impressed on the firmament, much more has the latter a seal of unfading perpetuity,—even Jesus high in the glories of heaven. Thus faith sees the Bow in the cloud, and adores the Saviour on the right hand of God.

But this is not all. The Bow, which cheers us in the first pages of our Bible, shines brightly to the last. We read in the Revelation, that John was in the Spirit;—a door was opened before him in heaven;—and, behold, a throne was set. But what encircled it? The Rainbow, Rev. iv. 3. As the vision advanced, he saw a mighty angel come down from heaven clothed with a cloud, and a rainbow was upon his head, Rev. x. 1. Thus in the fullest blaze of the Gospel, the Bow continued the chosen emblem of the grace and truth, which came by Jesus Christ.

How can we render thanks enough for this super-added pearl in our diadem of encouragements? We are thus led to look for our Bow on the brow of every threatening storm. In the world of nature it is not always visible: but in the world of grace it ever shines. When the darkest clouds thicken around us, the Sun of Righteousness is neither set nor has eclipse: and its ready smile converts the drops into an arch of peace.

Let a few cases from the diary of experience illustrate this. In our journey through the wilderness, the horizon is often obscured by storms like these; terrors of conscience,—absence of peace,—harassing perplexities,—crushing burdens of difficulties. But from behind these dusky curtains, the Bow strides forth in its strength.

It is indeed a cheerless day, when terrors of conscience pour down pitiless peltings. Spectres of past sins start up. A grim array of bygone iniquities burst their tombs; and each terrifies by hideous form, and each points to eternal death as its due. The light of life seems excluded by the dread, Can there be hope, when sins have been so many, and so grievous,—and against the clearest knowledge,—and after such tender pardons, and such healings of mercy? Wild is this tempest's roar: —but in its midst faith can still look upwards, and see Jesus with outstretched arms before the throne of God. There is a rainbow upon His Head, and the bright colours write, "Father, forgive them." "The blood of Jesus Christ His Son cleanseth us from all sin." The darkness vanishes, and clear joy returns.

Absence of peace, too, is a heavy cloud. Many a cross of spiritual distress lies in the believer's path. To-day he may recline joyously on the sunny slopes of the Gospel:—to-morrow the thunders of Sinai affright. To-day David sits high at the banquet of the king—to-morrow he is an outcast in the cave of Adullam. Now the Church rejoices in the voice of her Beloved, that knocketh, saying, "Open to me:"—soon she laments, "I sought Him, but I could not find Him." I must not pause to explore the marshes, from which these chilly mists arise. But it is sure, that the fault is with our hearts. Sin may be indulged:—then comforts die. Means of grace may be neglected:—then heavenly communions are shut out. But in these dreary hours the gladdening Bow, which crowns the Redeemer's head, will suddenly appear. In letters of light the truth is emblazoned, "Jesus Christ, the same yesterday, and to-day, and for ever." "I change not, therefore are ye not consumed." "I will never leave thee nor forsake thee." Again the darkness vanishes, and clear joy returns.

Perplexities are often as a mass of clouds. The pilgrim would climb the hill of Zion, but impassable rocks are on either side: —the sea is in the front: —the Egyptians in the rear. He sighs, as the lepers of Samaria, "If we say, we will enter into the city, then the famine is in the city, and we shall die there. And if we sit still here, we die also," 2 Kings, vii. 4. He is in the straits of David. The enemy has left him desolate; his friends are ready to stone him, 1 Sam. xxx. 6. But he looks aloft to Jesus, and the Bow is bright. The "faithful and true Witness" cheers him onward: "This is the way, walk in it." "I will instruct thee and teach thee in the way which thou shalt go, I will guide thee with mine eye."

So, also, burdens of difficulties often oppress. The believer is ready to sink beneath the weight. Moses felt this when he said, "Who am I, that I should go unto Pharaoh, and that I should bring forth the children of Israel?" But a Bow was in the cloud, and it sparkled with the promise, "Certainly I will be with thee." He went and prospered. The women on the way to the sepulchre were in gloom, "Who," said they, "will roll us away the stone?" But a Bow was in the cloud. Hoping against hope, they advanced, and the stone was gone. Paul trembled, when he was to stand alone before the tyrant and his court. But a Bow was in the cloud, and he took courage: "At my first answer no man stood with me, but all men forsook me. Notwithstanding the Lord stood with me, and strengthened me, and I was delivered out of the mouth of the lion."

Believer, have you, like Noah, been called by God into the ark of Salvation? Then, like Noah, you may trace the Bow in every trial and discouragement. Go forward undismayed, for you are encompassed with heaven's hosts of covenant-grace. Nothing can separate from the love of God, which is in Christ Jesus. You believe that no waters can again destroy this earth. So believe, that neither sin, nor Satan can sweep you to perdition. Your "life is hid with Christ in God." The eternal God is your tower of security. The arms of Christ are the guards around you. While God is God, mightier than Satan, you are safe. While Christ is Christ, all-sufficient to redeem, you are safe. Behold the Bow. Satan cannot pluck it from the skies. Behold your Jesus. Satan cannot reach His throne.

But do not extol the beauties of the Bow, who are strangers to the sheltering ark? Alas! it is no harbinger of peace to such. It tells indeed, that God is love, and God is true. But love rejected is no friend: and truth unheeded is a relentless foe. When the clouds blacken, let such tremble:—for truth says, "upon the wicked He will rain fire and brimstone, storm and tempest." When the Bow gleams sweetly forth, let them tremble:—for it warns, God has set me here as a pledge, that His word cannot be broken.

Believer, these lines guide you to look upward; may they also help you to look onward! Here you have no Bow without a cloud and without a storm. Here you see Jesus only by the eye of faith, in emblems, in records, and in means of grace. But soon, throughout eternity's calm brightness, you will gaze upon the Bow of His glory. And as you gaze, you will shine, even as He shines. For we shall be like Him, when we shall see Him as He is, 1 John iii. 2.

THE BLESSING

"In thee shall all families of the earth be blessed."—
GEN. xii. 3.

OUR Heavenly Father is love. The proof is the gift of His Son. Jesus is love. The proof is the gift of Himself. The Spirit is love. The proof is, He brings Jesus into the heart of faith.

Hence, the Scripture is framed by the hand of love, as a chart to show the glories of the Lord to the children of men. Each page adds new tints to the glowing picture. Almost each person is a herald preceding Jesus with a clearer note. Thus Abraham appears from the shades of idolatry, and instantly the Gospel is preached, Gal. iii. 8. The tidings sound aloud,—" In thee shall all families of the earth be blessed." Faith hears and cries, This must be a prophecy of Jesus. Who but He is the blessing of the world?

When the Patriarch was raised to this pinnacle of truth, what prospects, as floods of light were spread before him! He gazed on countless masses of immortals, blessed through countless ages. "Your father Abraham rejoiced to see my day, and he saw it, and was glad," John viii. 56.

Reader, would you behold like wonders, and share like joys? Would you be blessed while you live, and when you die, and throughout eternity? Would you bask each day in the smiles of God's favour, and repose each night under the shelter of His wings, and go down to the grave leaning on His arm, and pass through the gate of death into the new Jerusalem?—There is all this blessedness in Christ.

Would you at each moment lift up a tranquil heart, and say,—The great Creator is my Father:—Jesus is my redeeming kinsman;—the Spirit is my indwelling teacher, and sanctifier, and comforter;—the saints in light are my brethren;—the Angels are my guardian-attendants;—Heaven is my home;—a throne of glory is my seat;—a weight of glory is my crown? Would you realise, that the wheels of Providence revolve for your welfare;—and that the world, with all its intricate perplexities of machinery, is a scaffold to build up the fabric of your best interests? There is all this blessedness in Christ.

But apart from Him, there is no blessing. The blessing hand hangs down, the blessing voice is mute, except in Him. Such is the fact; and the clear knowledge of it lies at the root of Gospel-truth.

Do you ask, Wherefore can no blessing fly to earth, but on the wings of Jesus? Sin is the hindrance. Sin chokes the road. Blessings can find no channel, until some mighty power clears the course.

But sin does more than obstruct. It mantles our race under a thick pall of curse. The curse is the ground, on which we are born. On that dreary waste, then, nothing but woe can fall. We must be translated into an Eden of Grace, before showers of favour can visit us.

Many sport through life, thoughtless that they are thus in misery's land. As you value your soul, examine then with me the solemn case. Let us put aside all the false

maxims of the world. Let the childish conceits of puny
reason hide their heads. Let the Word speak from its
lofty and infallible tribunal.

Its sentence is most clear. No dulness can mistake it.
No guile can obscure it. The Lord thus decides, " Cursed
is every one, that continueth not in all things, which are
written in the Book of the Law to do them," Gal. iii. 10.
Tremendous voice! Sinner! is it not an arrow through
your conscience? It speaks of you, for it includes " every
one." The net encompasses the whole family of man.
Neither the riches of the rich, nor the poverty of the
poor; neither the greatness of the great, nor the lowliness
of the lowly; neither the age of the aged, nor the youth
of the youthful; neither the learning of the learned, nor
the polish of the polite, nor the ignorances of the un-
tutored, are a door of escape. No condition, no qualities,
no attainments can extricate. All born of woman, in
every clime, and in every age, are fast bound by the
dread sentence.

Do you further ask, What is this edict of the Law? Its
one straight rule is love. This is its one requirement.
But the width goes widely over every thought; the length
is as long as all time. It says, Love God, love man, in
every movement of mind, in every period of being. Love
God, love man, perfectly, without faltering, without a
pause.

What if there be failure? Then comes the stern
penalty, " Cursed art thou." There is no place for ex-
cuse, nor for tears, nor for penitence, nor for prayers, nor
for promises of reform. Disobedience is Curse.

Turn not from this honest dealing. But rather mark,
how the work affects yourself. Do I add to Scripture?

Your answer must be, No. Do I magnify? How can terrors be added to what is infinitely terrible? How can unutterable awe be made more awful? Look around your frightful cell. The wall has no crevice. It is high; you cannot scale it. It is broad; you cannot find its boundary. From all points the thunder roars, "Cursed art thou."

But what is the curse? It is the endless accumulation of all the miseries which God's resources can command, and God's power can inflict. It is the fiery torrent from the lake of fire. It is pain which cannot be keener. It is despair which cannot be blacker. It is anguish which cannot be more bitter. It is eternity in the oneness of all torment. It is Hell.

Reader, such is the fearful state of all who have never fled from Sinai's terrors, and who die unblest with Sion's saving mercies.

But wherefore have I led you unto this fearful vale? It is, that you may look up to Jesus, "leaping upon the mountains, skipping upon the hills" of Blessing. If there be curse in the Law, wide and relentless, there is blessing in Him, co-extensive and co-eternal. He abolishes the curse. He crowns himself with thorns, that He may crown His people with glory.

He transacts this gracious work in the garden and on the cross. But how? Not by denying any claim. Not by suing for mitigation. Not by pleading extenuations. Not by asking clemency. Nay, He honours and magnifies the law to the uttermost. He glorifies the command as just, and righteous, and good. He grants, that the curse is fully merited, and that it must be fully borne.

Let it, then, all descend, He cries, but not on the poor

sinner. I offer Myself, as substitute, to endure the whole,
and upon Him the whole is poured. He is made a curse
for us. The sword of vengeance to the very hilt is
sheathed in His breast. The last dreg of wrath is drained
by Him. Not one drop remains for those whom He
represents. Thus He takes all the curse out of the hands
of God, and stands the one Blessing of the world.

Fain would I invite you to adore with me our Blessing
of blessings. But before such glories, all thoughts and
words are the shadows of a shade. Is freedom a blessing
to a pining prisoner; and the sovereign's pardon to a convicted traitor; and the endearments of his native land to
a returning exile? Is ease a blessing to the pain-racked,
and the voice of health to the wasted in sickness, and
opening sight to the sightless? Is comfort a blessing to
the comfortless,—rest to the weary,—a home to the houseless,—bread to the famished,—peace to the fearful? This
is but a faint outline of the blessings which abound in
Jesus.

It would be joy to roam over all the Scriptures, which
re-echo these tidings. But one brief notice must suffice.
"Blessed be the God and Father of our Lord Jesus
Christ, who hath blessed us with all spiritual blessings in
heavenly places in Christ," Eph. i. 3. The saying is one,
but it leaves nothing unsaid.

Survey this treasure-house of grace; how rich! how
full! The believer may say, This heritage is all my own.
Measure, if it be possible, the golden chain, which extends from one hand of God in eternity past to the other
in eternity to come. Every link is a Blessing.

Behold the starry canopy. The glittering orbs out-
shine all beauty, and exceed all number. Such is the

firmament of Christ. It is studded with blessings. But millions of worlds are less than the least; and millions of tongues are weak to tell them. Mark how they sparkle in the eye of faith. There are constellations of pardons. "In Him we have redemption through His blood, even the forgiveness of sins." There is the bright shining of adoption into the family of God. "As many as received Him, to them gave He power to become the sons of God." There is the milky-way of peace,—perfect peace, —heaven's own peace. "Peace I leave with you, my peace I give unto you." There is the morning-star of sin destroyed. "God, having raised up His Son Jesus, sent Him to bless you in turning away every one of you from his iniquities." There is the lustre of divine Righteousness. "This is His name, whereby He shall be called, The Lord our Righteousness." There is the light of life. "I give unto them eternal life." There is all glory. "The glory which Thou gavest me, I have given them." There is the possession of all present, and the promise of all future good. "All things are yours,"—"things present —things to come." There is the assurance, that nothing shall harm. "All things work together for good to them that love God, to them who are the called according to His purpose."

Such is the blaze of Blessings, on which the believer calmly gazes. But are they yours? They are, if you have found refuge in the ever-blessing arms of Jesus. If not, take warning! Yours is the starless night of the terrific curse.

Perhaps I address some minister of the Lord. Sir, like Jesus, you are set for the falling and rising again of many. If you would happily work happiness, tell your flock of

Him. Preach Him clearly—fully—only—in season—out of season. Guide from the wilderness of the curse to the only pastures in which true Blessings can be gathered.

Do I address a parent? You love your children. With yearning heart, and tearful eye, you often sigh, Oh that the Lord would bless them indeed! Teach them Christ. Other instruction, if He be omitted, only adds sting to the curse, and accomplishes for hell.

Reader, you have friends dear to you as life. To advance their interests you count all labours light. Remember, he is a foe who befriends not the soul. To befriend the soul is to point it to Christ.

Perhaps you occupy a position of responsibility. You have dependents in the family—the trade—the shop— the farm. You feel for their comfort, and you provide for it. They look to you for support, and you give it. This is so far well. If this world were all, you would be a Blessing to them. But the world beyond the grave is all. Therefore to be a Blessing to them, you must win them to the knowledge, and faith, and love, and service of Jesus.

But perhaps you are of humbler station. Be it so. Some of the Lord's most successful labourers were poor, yet making many rich. You have a tongue, which daily utters many words. Each word enters some ear, and may enter some heart. Be persuaded then, and let your lowly words minister grace and blessedness, by being channels to convey the salvation of Jesus.

Whoever you are, turn not then from these earnest truths, until the Spirit bear witness with your spirit, that the one Blessing of all the families of the earth is the Blessing of your heart. Abide in Him; and the Blessing of the friend of God is yours. "I will bless thee, and thou shalt be blessed."

But the full grant of blessedness cannot be imagined, until His own welcome be heard, "Come, ye blessed of my Father, inherit the kingdom prepared for you from the foundation of the world."

MELCHIZEDEK

"Melchizedek, king of Salem, brought forth bread and wine, and he was the priest of the most high God."—GEN. xiv. 18.

THE first war, which darkens history's page, is ended. Abraham is moving homewards—crowned with success—laden with spoil. Suddenly a scene breaks on us —marvellous in what it reveals—marvellous in what it conceals. A personage, who is all wonder, stands on the stage of Scripture. His name bids us mark him well. It is a full Gospel-note. He is high in earthly dignity, for he is Salem's king. He is high in holy function, for he is the priest of the most high God. Do we ask his lineage? It is shrouded in a veil, which we may not pierce. Do we seek the morning of his days? His sun never rises. Do we seek the evening of his life? His sun never sets. He only appears in full-blown stature, and in meridian blaze. So obscure is he in sublimity, so sublime in obscurity, that it is no surprise to hear the question, Can this be merely man? He comes forward with neither empty hand nor silent lip. He strengthens the patriarch with refreshment for the way. He adds, too, the greater strength of blessing in the name of God. Abraham owns the claim to reverence and to homage. He presents a tenth part of all.

Such is the record. But Scripture pauses not here. It teaches us, that all these lines of mystery are lineaments

106

of Jesus. It shows, in this stately person, no doubtful glimpse of the glories of the office of the Lord. It tells us in distinct phrase, he is "made like unto the Son of God," Heb. vii. 3. The tidings are oft repeated, that Jesus is "a priest for ever after the order of Melchizedek." Hence faith, which only lives looking unto Jesus, sits at His feet in holy, happy musings, and finds the cheering of full Gospel-rays.

Behold Melchizedek! In wise purpose his descent is hid far beyond our sight. So, too, clouds and darkness mantle the first rise of Jesus. He is, by eternal generation, the co-eternal Son of the co-eternal Father. But who can grasp such mystery? He, who begets precedes not the begotten. He, who is begotten, is not second to the parent-cause. This truth is a boundless ocean. Let us meekly stand on the shore and marvel. But let us not repine, that we cannot fathom what is fathomless. This truth hides its lofty summit in the heaven of heavens. Let the poor worms of earth repose in reverence around the base. But let them not venture to climb the giddy heights. To know God's essence, we must have God's mind. To see Him as He is, we must be like Him. To span the lengths of His nature, we must have His infinitudes. To survey His amplitudes, we must sit as compeers on His throne.

We read, and are assured, that Jesus, by eternal birth, is God of God, and very God of very God. But while we cannot dive into the depths, we bathe our souls in the refreshment of the surface. For hence it follows, that He is sufficient to deal with God ,and to satisfy God, and thus to save His people to the uttermost. We see not Melchizedek's cradle. But we distinctly see him man on earth. Eye-witnesses, who heard Jesus and handled Him, give testimony, that He, too, has tabernacled in our clay, and thus was qualified to shed His life-blood as our ransom.

In Melchizedek we find neither first nor latest hours. No search can tell when he began or ceased to be. Here is Jesus. His age is one everlasting day. From eternity past to eternity to come, His being rolls in one unbroken stream. Before time was, His name is, " I am that I am." When time shall have run its course, His name is still, " I am that I am."

Reader, does such greatness fill you with tremblings of awe? Do you sigh, How can I draw near? How can I cast myself into His arms? Behold Him. His eternal being is eternal love. He never lived, He never will live, but with His people engraven on His heart, and spread before His eye. "I have loved thee with an ever-lasting love; therefore with loving-kindness have I drawn thee." Zion's walls are continually before Him. Immeasurableness encourages, for it is immeasurableness of tender grace.

Melchizedek. How mighty is this name! He that utters it, says, King of Righteousness. Who can claim that title, in its full purport, but Jesus; What is His person, what His work, but the glory of Righteousness? Since Adam fell, earth has seen no Righteousness apart from Him. But His kingdom is first Righteousness, then Peace, Rom. xiv. 17. There is a throne in it righteously erected to dispense Righteousness. All the statutes—decrees—ordinances—every precept—every reward—every penalty—is a sunbeam of Righteousness. Each subject is bright in royal robes of purity—each wears a crown of Righteousness, 2 Tim. iv. 8. Each delights in Righteousness, as his new-born nature.

Reader, do you not long to be righteous, even as He is righteous? There is one way—only one. Cleave to Jesus. His Spirit-giving sceptre will kill in you the love of sin, and plant in you the living seeds of Righteousness.

Melchizedek was a local monarch. His city was graced with the name of Salem, which is Peace. The war, which stalked through the land, troubled not these tranquil citizens. Here again we have the sweet emblem of Jesus' blissful reign. His kingdom is one atmosphere of peace: —one haven of unruffled calm.

Heaven is at peace with the inhabitants. Sin had rebelled. It had aroused most holy wrath. It had armed each attribute of God with anger. It had unsheathed the sword of vengeance. It had pointed the arrows of destruction against our world of transgression. But Jesus cleanses His flock from every stain of evil. He is "The Lamb of God, which taketh away the sin of the world." The eye of God can no more find the cause of enmity. A flood of smiles descends upon the blood-washed kingdom.

The inhabitants are at peace with heaven. Sin had filled them with hatred of God's holiness—dread of God's avenging arm—aversion to God's presence. But Jesus, by His Spirit, plucks out the heart of stone, and implants a heart of filial love. The one delight is now to draw near to God—to walk by His side—to listen to His voice —to sing His praise.

The inhabitants are at peace within. The sight of

the cross stills each rising storm of conscience, and stifles the accusing voice of Satan. They see a divine Redeemer quenching by His blood the flames of hell—building by His merits the palace of heaven. Trouble vanishes before this morning star.

Reader, there is no peace but in this Salem. But within these walls there is one song of perfect peace. The gates are yet wide open. The Prince of Peace calls to His standard. Blessed, blessed are they, who hear, and hasten, and are at rest!

Melchizedek is called to the most hallowed functions. He is the consecrated priest of the most high God. As king, he sat above men. As priest, he stands before God. This holy office exhibits Jesus. He spurns no office which can serve the Church. The entrance of sin calls for expiation. No sinner can approach a sin-hating God without a sin-removing plea. This expiation can only be by the death of an appeasing victim. The victim can only die by a sacrificing hand. Hence we need a Priest to celebrate the blood-stained rite. And all which is needed, we have in Jesus. Cry out and shout, O happy believer, your " Christ is all."

An altar is upraised. The altar is Christ. No other can suffice. He alone can bear the victim, which bears His people's sins. A lamb is led forth. The lamb is Christ. None other has blood of merit co-equal with man's guilt. Jesus, therefore, God in essence, man in person, extends himself upon the accursed tree. But who is the Priest who dares approach a super-human altar? Who has a hand to touch a victim-God? The very sight would shiver man into annihilation. Therefore Jesus is the Priest.

But can He slay Himself?

Reader, God's will is His nature. Love for His people is His heart. He looks to God—He looks to His Church, and counts it joy to give His blood. Believer, open wide your eyes of faith: gaze on this glorious work of your glorious High Priest. He spares not Himself, that all who flee to Him, might be spared for ever.

But mark it well, the Lamb has died once and for ever. The Priest's work on earth is finished once and for ever. The shadows are passed away. The one Priest has entered with His own blood into the holy of holies, having obtained eternal redemption. Will any now speak of priests, and altars, and sacrifices on earth? Let them beware. Let them consider. It is no light matter to trifle with the Spirit's language, and the names of Jesus. What begins in ignorance may end in death. "It is finished," is gloriously inscribed on the Priest's work below. "It never ceases," is as gloriously written on the work above. Jesus lives and His office lives Believer, behold Him on the right hand of the Majesty on high. He appears in priestly vesture. The names of the true Israel are on His shoulders,—a token, that all His strength is theirs to uphold them. The names are on His breast,—a token, that, while His heart beats, it beats for them. The voice of His pleading ever sounds and ever prevails. Father, forgive them; and they are forgiven. Father, have mercy on them; and mercies speed on rapid wing. The incense of His intercession ever rises. Father, bless them; and they are blessed. Father, smile on them; and it is light around. With extended hand, He takes their every offering of prayer, and praise, and service.

He perfumes all with the rich fragrance of His merits. He makes all worthy in His own worthiness, and thus our nothingness gains great reward.

Melchizedek meets Abraham with bread and wine. The weary warrior is way-worn and faint. Refreshment is provided. The Lord is very tender of His people's need. Awful is the curse on the Ammonites and the Moabites, because they met not Israel with bread and water in the way, when they came forth out of Egypt, Deut. xxiii. 4. Here again we see our great High Priest. With God-like bounty, He presents every supply, which wasted strength, and sinking spirits, and failing heart require. The fight of faith is fierce: the journey of life ofttimes seems long: but at every step a banquet-house is open, and recruiting delights are spread. There is the solid sustenance of the Word: there are the overflowing cups of the promises: there is the abundant feast of holy ordinances: there are the Sacraments, as manna from the hand of God: there is the spiritual food of His own body given,—of His own blood shed. Our true Melchizedek invites us to draw near. And while we regale in soul-reviving faith, the gracious voice still sounds, "Blessed be thou of the most High God."

The Patriarch, in grateful reverence, makes an offering of a tenth part of all. O my soul, what will you render to your great High Priest? Let your adoring language be, O Lord, I am Thine: Thou hast bought me by Thy blood: Thou hast won me by Thy melting grace: Thou hast called me by Thy constraining voice: Thou hast subdued me by Thine all-conquering Spirit. I am Thine. My soul is Thine to adore Thee: my heart is

Thine to love Thee: my body is Thine to serve Thee:
my tongue is Thine to praise Thee: my life is Thine to
glorify Thee; mine eternity is Thine to gaze on Thee
—to follow Thee—to hymn Thy name. But Eternity—
Eternity—Eternity is too scanty for a redeemed soul to
magnify a redeeming Jesus!

THE SHIELD

"Fear not, Abram: I am thy Shield."—GEN. xv. 1.

ABRAHAM had heard the terrible clang of war. He had been in perils of fight. Thus he knew, that without the safeguard of a Shield, the warrior must go forth to overthrow and death.

The sword was scarcely sheathed, when the Lord, remembering His mercy, visits His faithful servant. Seasonable are His words of comfort. "Fear not, Abram, I am thy Shield." Here was assurance, that all foes were as chaff: for the patriarch was encompassed with God, as with a buckler.

In Abraham warring, and Abraham shielded, every soldier of the blessed Jesus sees himself. The service of the Lord, soothed as it is with heaven's own peace, is still a storm of assaults from earth and hell. The repose of faith excludes not the fight of faith. Rest in trouble is not rest from trouble. Hostile bands must meet us in hostile land. Satan is yet at large, and is full of wrath. The flesh is still the flesh, and lusts against the spirit. The world is still the world; and, though worn out by centuries of sin, is vigorous to hate, apt to wound, powerful to captivate, strong to enchain. Hence a ceaseless tide of battle rolls. But it is vain, for Jesus ever lives, and ever loves, and still cheers every believer, saying, " Fear not, I am thy shield."

But what is a shield? It is armour framed for defence. Borne on the arm of the combatant, by rapid movement, it baffles the assailant's aim. Whatever be the attack, its broad surface intervenes, and all behind is safe. Just so in the fierce battle-field of faith, Jesus is a wide-spread covering. Hence every foe hurls every dart, as an innocuous reed.

Reader, here is a holy image. May it speak holy lessons to the soul! It will do so, if by the Spirit's life-giving grace, it makes Jesus more clear to faith, more dear to the heart. Let us then take our prayerful stand on the ground of truth, and solemnly mark what perils threaten, and how Jesus wards them off.

How few duly consider the tremendous dangers, to which they are exposed by sin! Could the monster be so lightly regarded, so trifled with, so fondled, if its nature and its consequences were really seen? Could men so live in its embrace, if they felt that it makes God an enemy? But truly it girds God, and all that God is, with weapons of just wrath. The thunderbolts of divine fury burn hot against it. The right arm of omnipotent displeasure is ever raised to sweep it to destruction.

Such is the awful fact. But how can dust and ashes stand, when God arises in the magnitude of infinite vengeance, and in the multitude of infinite resources? Flight there is none, for God is everywhere. Resistance there is none, for God has all power. Self is ruin, because self is sin: and sin is the only cause of the ire.

But do I in these pages converse with any one who is most righteously provided in Christ Jesus.

He stands between the justly-offended majesty of God, and the justly-perishing offender. He presents Himself to receive each blow. They fall, they all fall, they all must fall. Truth and holiness require it. But they fall, they all fall, on Him. Terrible is the outpouring of the indignation, which beats terribly against Him. " It pleased the Father to bruise Him." But He bears all.— If Deity assails, Deity sustains. It is against His fellow, that Jehovah wakes His sword. All the arms of the armoury of an avenging God fall harmless, because all spend their fury in the breast of God's co-eternal and co-almighty Son. Thus the believer meets God's wrath, and lives.

Reader, are you safely hid in Jesus? Woe is merited by you, and it must come. To brave it in the open plain of defenceless nature is sure perdition. There is no shadow of safety, but under these sheltering wings. Have you by faith made this refuge yours? Faith, and faith only, admits into the impenetrable defence. " Being justified by faith, we have peace with God through our Lord Jesus Christ."

But God's abhorrence of evil is not our only adversary. There is the evil one, red with the blood of myriads of our race. He cannot but hate, for his heart is hatred. He cannot pity, for he revels in man's misery. He cannot spare, because he lives, when we die. The first days of our pilgrimage are the first days of his plots,—his wiles,—his cruel warfare. He lays an ambush at every turn. Now a shower of darts pelts pitilessly. Now the weight of incessant batterings descends. Now a sudden arrow flies swiftly in the dark; and suddenly we fall, ere danger is suspected. He never slumbers, never is weary, never relents, never abandons hope. He deals his blows alike at childhood's weakness, youth's inexperience, manhood's strength, and the totterings of age. He watches to ensnare the morning thought. He departs not with the shades of night. By his legions he is everywhere, at all times. He enters the palace, the hut, the fortress, the camp, the fleet. He invests every chamber of every dwelling, every pew of every sanctuary. He is busy with the busy. He hurries about with the active. He sits by each bed of sickness, and whispers into each dying ear. As the spirit quits the tenement of clay, he still draws his bow with unrelenting rage.

Such is our terrific and life-long fight. How can it be that each moment is not a death-wound? We could not but be cast down, except some Shield, far stronger than our own struggles, or our own resolves, were cast around us. And where can we find this shelter, but in Jesus?

He interposes the might of His intercession: "Simon, Simon, behold, Satan hath desired to have you, that he may sift you as wheat, but I have prayed for thee, that thy faith fail not." His prayers are our victory. They gain supplies of divine aid. They brace us with heaven's strength. Thus we resist the devil, and he flees from us.

Jesus shields us, too, by giving the Shield of faith. He is the author and finisher of this grace. Against this all the fiery darts of the wicked are powerless. They touch it, only to be quenched.

The sprinkling of His blood is also an impregnable security. Satan sees this and trembles. It is mail, which he cannot pierce. This is the one experience of the Church of the firstborn. They are all sorely pressed, but they are more than conquerors, for they overcome by the blood of the Lamb. Thus the Evil One touches not the shielded ones of Jesus.

But there are other foes swarming in every secret corner of the camp. We have to wrestle with self, which cleaves to us as a girdle of destruction. The flesh gives no quarter. Its lusts are terrible shafts. They have strewn the earth with heaps of mighty slain. David met them without his Shield, and his scar went down with him to the grave. Joseph was assailed. The enemy's aim was skilful, and bold, and strong. But the Lord covered his heart, and temptation entered not. "How," said he, "can I do this great wickedness, and sin against God?" The blow recoiled, and he was safe.

The pleasures, too, the luxuries, the honours of high station, beat down their countless victims. None can withstand them in human strength. And none can be vanquished, who have the Lord for their breastplate. Moses was tried by their most seductive craft. He might have sat next to the king in royal state. But he "endured, as seeing Him who is invisible." And being dead, he tells us, how to drive back this wily troop of fascinations.

Man's frown and persecution's threat give deadly wounds. All this fury affrighted Daniel and the captive youths. The tyrant's wrath, the burning fiery furnace, the den of raging beasts gaped menacingly on them. But they fled to the Lord. He was their Shield, and they were unharmed in spirit and in body.

Moreover, the Zion-ward path is in the face of batteries, from which hosts of cares and anxieties pour down their envenomed darts. How suddenly will they muster their efforts to disquiet! It is well with me to-day through grace. But what may come on the morrow? Friends may fail. Their pleasant seats may be a melancholy void. Disease and languishings may make the frame a misery. Such thoughts are pointed with keen anguish. And there is no shelter, but in the Lord. He alone can deaden their sting. But He can shield by spreading before our eyes His eternal love, His never-failing presence, His ever-watchful care, His ever-living promises. No apprehensions can slay the life, or vigour, or calm of the soul, when the voice of Jesus whispers, "Fear thou not, for I am with thee." "All things are yours." "This God is our God for ever and ever, He will be our guide even unto death." The soul is surely cased in peace, when it is folded in the arms of Jesus.

Reader, are you a true disciple of this Lord? If so, bring forth your trial, your foe, your peril, your need, and I will show you Jesus Almighty, and immovable, and ever-watchful to screen you from this very hurt. "The name of the Lord is a strong tower; the righteous runneth into it and is safe."

But do I in these pages converse with any one who is afar off from Christ? Unhappy child of man! can I speak to you of security? Nay, I warn you, that you are on all sides defenceless, and in the midst of ruins. Where is your shelter from the wrath of God? Where, from the rage of Satan? Where, from the death-blows of self? Where, from the soul-murdering world? You have none. Oh! think. It is not yet too late. You yet live, and your wounds, though many, may all be healed; and your foes, though many, may all be driven, like vanishing smoke, before you. The words, on which your eye now rests, direct you to the only refuge. Flee unto Jesus.

He is always near, and always sufficient to be your all-sufficient Shield.

Believer, will not you put your seal to this truth? Have you not found a panoply of aid in Him? Can you not say with David, "Many there be which say of my soul, there is no help for him in God. But Thou, O Lord, art a shield for me!" Will you not cry, "Happy art thou, O Israel! who is like unto thee, O people, saved by the Lord, the Shield of thy help, and the sword of thy excellency?" And will you not exhort, "O Israel, trust thou in the Lord, He is their help, and their Shield. O house of Aaron, trust in the Lord, He is their help and their Shield. Ye that fear the Lord, trust in the Lord, He is their help and their Shield."

What especial encouragement is here to the faithful minister of Christ! What a tower of all-prevailing strength to the humble labourers in the Gospel-field! They seem to sow in weakness the seed of a few weak words. But it takes root. A gracious plant springs up. It sheds forth fragrance like Eden, and bears fruit for the garner of the King of kings. It thus flourishes, though checked by ungenial climate—scorched by fiery suns— battered by rain and hail. The boar out of the wood cannot waste it; nor the wild beast of the field devour it. How is this? "Upon all the glory is a defence." No weapon, that is formed against it, can prosper; for the Word of the Lord is truth, "I am thy Shield."

Therefore, ye servants of the living God, bless His holy name. He always causes you to triumph in Christ. Go on with the shield of faith, and under the covering of your Lord. Soon will the conflict end: and in Salvation's kingdom you will sing the glories of Salvation's Shield.

THE EXCEEDING GREAT REWARD

"I am thy shield, and thy exceeding great reward."
—GEN. XV. 1.

IT is a grand truth, that pleasantness and peace hold constant court in the believer's breast. But it must be so. For where faith dwells, there is Christ; and He enters as the author and giver of all joy.

Reader, come apart for a little moment, and pray over the simple words, which here endeavour to confirm this principle. If the Christ-revealing Spirit withdraw the veil, you will see the well-spring of happiness. Drinking of this pure stream, you will go on your way, blessed with much of heaven in possession—with all heaven in prospect.

We here fly back to Abraham's inspiring annals. He was dwelling in the land of his birth, in the home of his childhood, amid the friends of his heart. A voice shakes him from his dead repose.

" Get thee out from thy country, and from thy kindred, and from thy father's house." Many would have said, " This is a hard saying, who can hear it?" Not so the called of the Lord. By faith he " obeyed, and he went out, not knowing whither he went." He was no loser. He received manifold more in this present time, and in the world to come life everlasting.

Again, when he had scattered kings in the rescue of Lot, princely treasures courted his acceptance. Masses of gold and silver sparkled at his feet. "Take the goods to thyself," was a tempting offer, but with holy indifference he turned away. He was no loser. After these things, an assurance richer than all the riches of earth enriched him. "Fear not, Abram, I am thy Shield and thy exceeding great reward."

Now in this narrative we have an unerring teacher's voice. It tells us that the true Christian is called to many relinquishments, to much self-denial, to constant trampling on earth's gilded baits. But it tells us, that every relinquishment is wealth, and every loss is gain. For he who leaves all for Christ, receives more than all in Christ.

A few particulars will establish this truth. There is a plain inscription over the portal of the heavenward-path: "Strait is the gate, and narrow is the way." He, then, who would enter, must be stripped of all those flowing robes, in which men flaunt and swell in nature's broad road. Self-righteousness must be torn off to its every shred. This is the very flaying of the soul. Dependence on fancied merit adheres as the very skin. But it all must yield. Self, in its most cherished form, must be despised and hated, as an abominable thing. All our darling excellences, all our fond conceits, all our superiorities must be rejected, as a filthy rag. It is hard work to cast all this away, and to go naked to be clothed by Jesus. But, if ever we would be saved, it must be done.

So, too, every hope, which finds a Saviour in the externals of rites and services, and means of grace, must be ground to powder and given to the winds. The channels of grace are not grace. The way is not the end. The implements, by which we feed, are not food. The husk is not the kernel. The casket is not the jewel. The scaffold is not the building. The door is not the mansion. Here again is work, which requires a martyr's spirit, and more than human discernment. Satan is quick to deck our holy things, and our holy places with a show of saving efficacy. He whispers, that to put these into their proper place, is to put religion out of all place.

But we must not hesitate. Christ must be embraced, unaided and alone, or not at all.

I need scarcely add, that every sweet sin, which has long been caressed in the recesses of the heart, must be dragged to the light and slain. This is ofttimes as the plucking out the right eye. But there must be no sparing. Christ is light. Sin is darkness. How can they be one? Sin loved, indulged, retained, binds fast the soul to the wheels of the chariot in which Christ cannot sit.

Again, the love of the world, in its foolish vanities, its empty shows, its godless maxims, its defiling pleasures, its lying principles, its soul-beclouding books, and all its idol-worship of talent, wit, and falsely-called glory, must be nailed to the cross. Its conformity must be eschewed, as poison—its touch shunned, as a viper's sting. The heart must have no throne, but for Christ. Every joy must centre in Him—every flower of refreshment must be gathered from Him. This walk is a departure from nature's country, from sin's kindred, and from the devil's home. It is a march towards a land, which Christ will give. It requires efforts many, and struggles many, and conflicts many, thus to take up the Christian's staff, and to put on the Christian's sandal, and to spurn all things dear to nature and to self.

But what is rejected? Nothing but husks and

shadows:—nothing but vexation, and disappointment, and misery:—nothing but an oppressive load, a mocking shadow, a gnawing care, a weary chase after emptiness, a groaning under present burden, a dread of future reckoning. What is gained? The substance of all good, the perfection of all excellence, in Christ. He welcomes to the secret chambers of His love. He opens His heart. A voice is heard by every coming sinner, You thus give yourself to Me, because I gave Myself for you, and now I give Myself to you. Fear not, I am your " exceeding great reward."

O my soul, is this all-satisfying treasure yours? It turns all dross to gold, all clouds to sunshine, all sighs to song, and earth to the very gate of heaven. Mark well the vast assurance, I am " thy exceeding great reward." There would have been wondrous grace in the word, I will give some recompence. But it is more than grace to say, I myself am your reward. The prospect of future glory would have been sweet encouragement? but it is mercy above mercy to bestow a present, instant privilege. I am your reward. There would have been marvellous comfort in the pledge, You shall lose nothing in my service. But it is very God to speak, I am " thy exceeding great reward." Mark, then, the vast assurance. Christ Himself is the reward—the present reward —the great reward—the exceeding great reward, which fills believing hearts. All He is, and all He has is theirs. Theirs by His love, which had no birth;—theirs by His grace, which has no bounds;—theirs by His promise, which has no change; theirs by His gift, which cannot be recalled. Theirs, because He delights to bless them. Theirs, because He overjoys in their joy.

Fain would I speak of the reward, which He gives in the gift of Himself. But here the tongues of men and angels fail.

He is God. Is His deity a treasure? He says to His people, Open wide your hands, My deity is yours. As God, His power is Omnipotence. He uses it for them. It protects them by night and day from the fury and hate of earth and hell. It stands every moment a high barrier between them and destruction. It prevails with Satan to beat him back. It prevails with the Father to draw Him near. His wisdom is unsearchable. But it is all for them. He so plans and disposes, that the fate of empires and the falling sparrow alike yield them good. His Spirit is theirs. He is sent forth to awaken, to reveal salvation, to win to the cross, to cheer, to sanctify, and to lead into the pastures of truth and holiness.

He is God-man. As such He has died, and endured agonies, and sustained a curse, and wrought righteousness, and possesses a kinsman's heart to sympathise. All is theirs. His death is theirs, that they may never die. His agonies are theirs, to expiate. His curse is theirs, to redeem. His blood is theirs, to wash them whiter than the whitest snow. His righteousness is theirs, to deck them in beauties meet for the Father's admiring gaze. His sympathy is theirs, that He may have a fellow-feeling in all their infirmities, and a brother's pity in all their griefs. So, too, His present life is theirs, that they may live for ever. His intercession is theirs. Hence streams of blessings ever flow. His advocacy is theirs. Hence pardons cease not: and God's countenance is ever the meridian-sun of smiles.

Yet a little while, and He comes again. His return

is theirs, to receive them in glorified bodies unto Himself. His heavens are theirs, that they may dwell in one home. His throne is theirs, that they reign on one seat. His angels are theirs, as ministering guards. His providences are theirs, always revolving around the pivot of their welfare. His ministers are theirs, to call, to feed, to build them up. His Scriptures are theirs, as a mirror, in which they may see His work and learn His ways. His ordinances are theirs, as nourishment and strength. His sacraments are theirs, as seals and pledges of His everlasting covenant. Thus they live, that they may receive grace from Him. They die, that they may receive glory in Him. They revive, that they may see all the perfections of Jehovah, and feast upon all joys before Him.

Reader, strive to expand these hints. They tend to show the blessedness of the "exceeding great reward" in Christ. But is it your desire to have your portion in such happy state? Come, then, surrender all for Christ. Make Him your own by faith. Lift up the gate of your heart, and this King of Glory will come in. Abide in Him, and He will abide in you. Give Him your confidence, and He will be to you this boundless recompence. Can you think, that He is less rich to bless now, than He was of old? Have His rewards lost one grain of their immeasurable greatness? It cannot be. Act the faith of Abraham, and you will hear as Abraham heard, and find as Abraham found, "I am thy exceeding great reward." You will testify, as grateful Jacob did, "God hath dealt graciously with me, and I have enough," or rather, "I have all things." You will experience with Moses, that the reproach of Christ is greater riches than the treasures of kingdoms. You will touch the chord of

David's harp, and sound aloud, " The Lord is the portion of my inheritance, and of my cup." Your overflowing heart will testify, that the half was not told you.

But we need not go back to the early records of faith to show that Christ is this " exceeding great reward." It is the one experience of all His servants. Many are cottages, in which, while penury frowns, the godly inmate smiles content, and sings the song of heaven over scanty fare. Many are the reviled and the oppressed, in whose mouth is neither railing nor complaint, but one meek utterance of praise. Many are the chambers of languishing and pain, in which the very groans are melodies of gratitude. Many are the beds of dying, in which death is abolished and peace triumphs. Faith can explain all this. It knows Him, who, by His presence, makes all burdens light—all sorrows joy. It is the Lord. He dwells there by faith. He is the " exceeding great reward."

Faith, too, can take wings and pierce the skies, and enter the home of the redeemed. What is that scene? Multitudes upon multitudes, with robes of white, and crowns of righteousness, and palms of victory, and songs of endless praise, follow the Lamb withersoever He goeth. This is the recompence of Christ. He bought it all. He gave it all. He prepared it all for them. He prepared them all for it.

Is He not an " exceeding great reward?" Can you now take the world instead of Him? Look again. Read again . Think again. Holy Spirit! suffer no one to put these pages aside, until, by Thy mighty power, Christ is established in the heart, as the " exceeding great reward."

THE COVENANT

> "*I will establish My Covenant between Me and
> thee, and thy seed after thee, in their genera-
> tions, for an everlasting Covenant.*"—GEN.
> xvii. 7.

READER, does your conscience certify, that you are
a true disciple of the Lord Jesus Christ? Have you
cast a helpless soul into His helpful arms? Have you
buried all your guilt and all your fears in the grave of
His wounds? By death unto sin, do you prove, that you
are crucified with Him? By life unto righteousness, do
you manifest the power of resurrection with Him? If
so, what cause have you to bless God that He breathed
the breath of life into your nostrils, and the Spirit of life
into your soul! For great are your privileges, rich is
your portion, bright are your prospects, sure is your inheritance. Your blessedness is summed up in the word,
the great God is your Covenant-Father.

Search your Bible. Study the charter of your heavenly
freedom. Read the title-deeds of your high estate. This
world's miser counts his gold, his jewels, and his fields.
Shall not the heir of two worlds know his imperishable
wealth?

Clasp especially to your heart the roll of blessings in
Jer. xxxi. 33, 34. They are sanctification of spirit—
adoption into God's family—divine light—and eternal
pardon. The believer may claim them all by covenant-

pledge. "This shall be the Covenant, that I will make with the house of Israel; after those days, saith the Lord, I will put My law in their inward parts, and write it in their hearts; and I will be their God, and they shall be My people. And they shall teach no more, every man his neighbour, and every man his brother, saying, Know the Lord: for they shall all know Me, from the least of them unto the greatest of them, saith the Lord: for I will forgive their iniquity, and I will remember their sin no more."

Few are the eyes, which are not dazzled, when such treasures shine, as fields of light, before them. Wondering thought will question, How can God the high,—the holy,—whose being is perfection,—whose home is eternity, contract with man, the low,—the vile,—the loathsome,—the offspring of the dust,—the fluttering insect of a moment? No monarch would make league with the base rebel in the dungeon. How then can the height of heaven thus descend to misery, disease, and filth?

When nature looks down to the pit, in which human nature grovels, impossibilities seem many. But still the fact is sure, God is in Covenant with every child of grace.

Let witnesses be called. First, let Abraham appear. He was born in sin,—prone to evil,—the child of wrath, laden with iniquity, just as we are. But his evidence asserts, that God thus communed with him. "As for Me, Behold My Covenant is with thee." "I will establish My Covenant between Me and thee and thy seed after thee."

Let David next be heard. By natural descent, he was as we are. But his truthful gratitude exclaims, "He hath made with me an everlasting Covenant, ordered in all things, and sure."

Thus far the point is clear. God covenants with man. But, perhaps some trembling believer may doubt, whether such grace extends beyond the favoured elders in the household of faith. Mercy speeds to give the reply, The Covenant is established with Abraham and his seed after him. And "if ye be Christ's, then are ye Abraham's seed, and heirs according to the promise," Gal. iii. 29. Reader, this truth is now resplendent as the sun in its brightness. It cannot be denied, that if you are Christ's, you are a covenant-child of God.

We are thus prepared to examine the nature of God's Covenant, in its conditions and confirmation.

The first step is to settle deeply in your mind, that this Covenant is no covenant of works. Once, indeed, such compact was proposed. "Do this," was the requirement. "Live," was the recompence. But it saw the light only to perish. Man placed it not in his heart, but beneath his feet. He touched it only to scatter it to the winds. The privilege was instantly forfeited. The voice which began in promise, ended in wrath. The beauteous column fell, never to rise again. The gracious page was torn, never to be re-written.

I fear, that there are many, who in the dark night of nature dream the idle dream, that this Covenant still lives, and that they shall live through it. But a broken reed is no stay. The sinking sand is no foundation. A violated treaty is no sound plea. It is a pitiable argument, I claim, because I have no claim. As well might the prodigal demand, Receive me again, because I am undutiful: or the rebel, Restore me, because I am a traitor: or the criminal, Acquit me, because I am guilty: or the debtor, Release me, because I am fraudulent.

Such are the delusions of those, who trust in a vanished Covenant. It began and ended in Adam. The strength of innocence could not hold it. How then can the weakness of guilt recover it, or the tongue of transgression plead it? But far different is the Covenant, which is the believer's safeguard. It is written in unfading letters of eternal love. It is based on the rock of changeless purpose. It is such, because " God hath commanded it for ever."

But whence its birth, its vigour, its undying freshness? It exists, it is strong, it is everlasting, because it is made with Jesus. He stands before God as the second Adam,— the head of a Spirit-born progeny. God commits to Him terms and promises for them. He binds Himself to terms and promises for them. Thus God pledges to them: Christ pledges for them. God stipulates; Christ undertakes.

But what are the conditions? God requires, that they be all cleansed from all sin—all clothed in all righteousness—all renewed in every faculty of soul and spirit. Christ is responsible for the full performance. God promises, that He will be their God. Christ promises, that they shall be His people. Such is the new Covenant —made and ratified in Christ.

Let us now sit down beneath the tree of Scripture, and catch some precious fruit, which falls into the lap of faith. What rich supplies come from Isaiah xlii. 6, and xlix. 8! Here Jehovah communes with His co-equal Son. We are brought into the council-chamber of eternity. God, in His majesty, says, " I, the Lord, have called Thee in Righteousness, and will hold Thy hand, and will keep Thee, and give Thee for a Covenant of the people." And again, " I will preserve Thee, and give Thee for a Covenant of the people." We are here bade to gaze on Jesus, as Himself the Covenant. And such He is: for it has no being, no continuance, no power but in Him. He is its essence, its reality, its fulness, its all. It is founded, erected, concluded in Him. No Christ, no Covenant. Receive Him, and it is yours in all its truth and riches. Reject Him, and you perish, because you have not the shadow of a plea.

He is the Covenant, because, as Jehovah's fellow, He designs it, and wills it, and orders it, and frames it, and accepts it. He is the Covenant, because, as God-man, He takes it into His own hand, and works out its every condition.

Receive next the evidence of Mal. iii. 1. "The Lord, whom ye seek, shall suddenly come to His temple, even the Messenger of the Covenant, whom ye delight in." Here Christ is the Messenger of this Covenant. But what is the office of a messenger? He conveys tidings from party to party. Just so, Jesus comes travelling in the greatness of His strength, flying on the wings of His love, hastening in the zeal of His heart to proclaim, that a Covenant is made, and to tell what the Covenant contains. In the Word, through His ministers, by sealing ordinances, He reads to us, line by line, the provisions of this charter. He shows us, as in a glorious mirror— God reconciled, peace established, all grace purchased, and heaven's portals opened. O my soul! has Jesus caused the sweet notes of this message to be the music of your holiest delights?

But the messenger flies back to the courts above, and gives report to His heavenly Father, These poor sinners have heard of Thy Covenant-grace; they have hid their faces in the dust of penitential shame; they have clasped the records with the eager hand of adoring faith; old things are passed away from them, all things are become new; out of darkness they are light: from hatred they are love: they are no more aliens, but children. O my soul! are you thus brought within the bonds of the Covenant?

Again, glean the tidings of Heb. vii. 22, "By so much was Jesus made a Surety of a better testament," or Covenant. Here Christ is the Surety of this Covenant. But what is the work of a Surety? He engages, that each party shall fulfil the contract. There was no surety in the Covenant of works, and it quickly failed. But here the God-man Jesus is the Surety. He is Surety for the Father. He is Surety for His people. I need not repeat what boundless blessedness the Father promises. All shall be given. Not one drop shall be withheld. The cup shall overflow. It must be, for Jesus is Surety. The conditions of believers are alike secure. They shall kneel in penitence; and live by faith; and cling to the refuge; and be fruitful trees of righteousness. In due time Jesus will call them all, and work in them to will and to do, and at last present them cleansed, and washed, and beautified, and sanctified, a glorious Church, not having spot or wrinkle or any such thing. The truth, the love, the power of the Surety will accomplish this.

What delights, too, flow from Heb. xii. 24! "To Jesus the Mediator of the new Covenant." As Mediator, He stands between God and man. He is one with God, and one with man. He places His hands on each. Thus they

become one in Him. Separation vanishes: union is
effected. Thus Covenant-blessings never fail to wing
their way from heaven. Thus the Covenant-incense of
holy love, and filial fear, and willing service never ceases
to ascend.

Feast, moreover, on the truth of Heb. ix. 15. " He is
the Mediator of the New Testament, that by means of
death, for the redemption of the transgressions which
were under the first Testament, they which are called,
might receive the promise of eternal inheritance."
Covenants of old were rendered valid by a victim's
blood. When God showed Abraham the Covenant of
grace, a smoking furnace, and a burning lamp passed
between the slaughtered limbs. Hence the everlasting
Covenant must be sealed with blood. An atoning, a
peace-making sacrifice dies. It is none other than the
Mediator Himself. The Father is well-pleased, and cries,
" My Covenant will I not break, nor alter the thing that
is gone out of my lips." The believer responds with overflowing praise, God is my Covenant-Father for ever and
ever. His Covenant is sure with me; by the Spirit's help,
my covenant shall be inviolate with Him.

Reader, is such the language of your thanks-giving and
thanks-living heart?

Many, alas! prefer to enter into treaty with the world.
Its easy terms are easily proposed. It demands compli-
ance with its fashions;—adoption of its principles;— put-
ting on its habits;—neglect of the Bible;—worship in
mere forms. It offers in return a full-frothed cup of
animal and mental joy. The deluded victims sign. They
take the tinsel-goblet. They drink nothing but the dregs
of disappointment and of shame.

Then comes the end. An eternity of woe puts a seal to the truth, that the friendship of the world is enmity with God.

Flee from this deceiving truce-breaker! Come out. Stand apart. Be separate. Lost souls discover too late that a league with the world binds them over to hell.

JEHOVAH-JIREH

" Abraham called the name of that place Jehovah-Jireh."—GEN. xxii. 14.

FAITH is the brightest star in the firmament of grace. High is its origin—for it is born in heaven. Lowly is its abode—for it dwells on earth in the hearts of the redeemed. Mighty are its deeds—for it prevails with God, and over sin and Satan. It treads down seeming impossibilities. It strides to victory over mountains of stupendous hindrance. It speeds to its haven through oceans, in which each billow is an overwhelming difficulty. It braces the Christian warrior for every combat—giving a shield to screen, and a sword to subdue. It has a keen eye to discern things invisible. It reads the mind of God, as written in the tablets of eternity—as emblazoned on the cross of Christ—as wrapt up in the folds of providence. It enthrones Jesus, as king of the inner man. It kindles and fans the flame of love. It opens the lips of prayer and praise. It turns the current of life into a strong stream of spiritual service. It endures, until the gates of light open at its touch. It only expires, when it sees the Lord face to face.

Should we not then earnestly covet this gift of gifts? Should we not prize it, as the treasure of treasures? Should we not boldly use it, as our best defence? Should we not seek it, as our truest wealth?

With this desire, come with me, and let us view faith's prowess in one of the noblest passages of Abraham's noble life. And may the Lord the Spirit so accompany us with His gracious teaching, that we may become heirs of the faith and blessedness of this heroic servant of the Captain of Salvation! God had looked on Abraham, when he was low in Satan's dungeon. He had called him from bowing down to stocks and stones to see the light of life. He had turned the darkest night into the lustre of truth. He had ofttimes shone around him in cheering communion. He had opened to his wondering gaze the unsearchable riches of redemption. He had given pledge, that the Saviour from on high should put on human nature in his family. Nature called hope of progeny an idle dream. But the Lord spake, and Isaac lived.

After such miracles of mercies, after such wondrous promises, and more wondrous fulfilments; "God did tempt Abraham." A trial was sent to test the reality and the strength of his grace.

Reader, faith untried, unprobed, unproved, is faith uncertain. The quality of the metal is ascertained, by what it can do and bear. The courage of the soldier is evidenced in the field. The depth of the root is shewn by resistance to the hurricane. It is a rock, if no lashing surges can move it. It is a good foundation, when no batterings shake the building.

But trials do more than search whether faith be deep-rooted. They also consolidate and invigorate it. The oft-strained sinew becomes more firm. The long-strained racer wins the prize. By exercise new powers expand and meeten for the wrestle.

Reader, if you are a parktaker of this blessed gift, think

it not strange, that you are called to breast the thwarting current of many an opposing wave. It is needful—it is right—it is good. The issue will be a richer harvest of assurance and delight. Lift up then the head, and " count it all joy, when ye fall into divers temptations."

But what furnace was ever hot, as that which burnished Abraham's faith? He was rejoicing in his child—the signal token of God's signal favour. Suddenly the voice, which had so often caused his heart to burn, freezes his heart to stone. " Take now thy son, thine only son Isaac, whom thou lovest, and get thee into the land of Moriah, and offer him there for a burnt offering upon one of the mountains which I will tell thee of." He hears, but can he hear aright? His fondest hopes become a ruin. The promise, dearer than life, withers as a blight-stricken bud. The tree which held salvation's seed, falls low. The channel of redemption's stream is choked. But God spake—that is enough. The command is from heaven—positive and clear. It cannot err.

Isaac may die, but faith dies not. It can reason, God has all wisdom, and power, and truth; " with Him is no variableness, neither shadow of turning." Clouds and darkness may shroud the event. But through clouds and darkness, the faithful word and the loving purpose will break forth, as a summer's morn. So Abraham rose up early, and hastened to do His will.

Let this example teach, that prompt obedience is the surest wisdom. God loudly addresses you in your Bible. He shews you the one path of life. He calls you to bring one sacrifice to Him in the arms of faith, and to offer one Lamb on one Altar. Rise up early and obey. To linger is to court ruin. Delay is the craftiest net of Satan. It is the terrible pitfall, out of which there are rare escapes. Many in torment will for ever rue the miserable hesitation, which ended in their miserable end. They tarried, but death tarried not. They paused, and the voice of mercy ceased. Commands unheeded are the common and the rapid road to hell.

For three days Abraham journeyed towards the appointed mount. This was large opportunity for unbelief to whisper many a dissuading thought. This was long time for the father's heart to ache. He looks on his child, and there is agony. He looks up to his God, and the agony melts into the calmness of unruffled peace. He turns to his child, and his foot would fain falter. He turns to his God, and the step is firm in resolute resolve.

Reader, faith is a persevering and unflinching grace. It holds fast by the Word—so it holds on—so it holds out.

But now every fibre of affection is wrung by the simple inquiry of his confiding Isaac, "My father, behold the fire and the wood, but where is the lamb for a burnt offering?" None can tell the anguish of such a moment, for none were ever pierced by such an arrow, but it laid open the recesses of his heart, only to show how faith there reigned. "My son, God will provide Himself a lamb for a burnt offering." Here is faith in its simple element of trust, and in its single consistency of acting. It totters not. Its stand is, as a giant's stand on earth: because its head towers above the skies, gazing upon God. It leaves the time, the place, the means, the method, the all to Him. So it goes forward. It knows, that God's leadings lead to God's glory. And God's glory is its happy paradise.

It was so. Isaac is bound. And must he really die? Faith stays not to inquire. He is laid upon the altar. The hand is stretched out. The knife is taken. The last moment is come. But the last moment is the fit time to crown faith with reward, and victory, and peace. The voice which bade, now forbids. He who said, "Take thou thy son," arrests by saying, "Lay not thine hand upon the lad."

Behold God's wondrous way. His word is honoured. Faith triumphs, and is honoured too. It is tried, and by the trial is confirmed and expanded.

The patriarch now begins a new life of heavenly joy. For the joy of Isaac born is nothing to the joy of Isaac restored. A giving God was love in the highest. A restoring God is love in higher heights. Nor is this all. A memorial is raised to cheer the faithful throughout all generations. Abraham called the name of that place Jehovah-jireh; as it is said to this day, "In the mount of the Lord it shall be seen."

Believer, this memorial proclaims the full provision, which is laid up in Jesus for His waiting people. They are indeed loved, and cared for, and enriched. Jehovah-jireh is this sweet mountain of spices, on the many slopes of which they delightedly recline, and find all blessings strewd around them.

These pages are written to exhort you to make this spot your daily and your holy pleasure-ground. Intimately acquaint yourself with these green pastures. Be assured, that here sufficiency abounds for you, while time shall be, and when time shall be no more;—sufficiency for every need of body and of spirit, which has been, or shall be, or can be.

I well know that your poverty is deep—your perils countless—your strength a quivering reed. But still you are rich, and safe, and strong; for Jesus changes all your broken and your empty cisterns into overflowing fountains of most suitable supply.

When you feel that the burden of your sins is intolerable, and pressing you to the lowest depths of the bottomless abyss, come to Jehovah-jireh. Your Jesus provides relief. His arm is the arm of Omnipotence. His shoulders are the shoulders of Deity. With strong hand He places all your guilt on Himself, and bears it away, and it is no more found.

When you sigh to be assured, that your every debt is paid, your every penalty endured, come to Jehovah-jireh. Jesus is made flesh, and become your nearest kinsman, that in your very nature, and in your stead, He may pay all, and suffer all.

When your soul is trembling and fluttering, as the dove among unsparing vultures, or the lamb before devouring wolves, come to Jehovah-jireh. Jesus presents aid in each trial, power for each duty, shelter in each storm. He is the high place, which the shafts of the foe cannot reach—the covert, which the storm cannot pierce. His sure voice proclaims, " I the Lord do keep it, I will water it every moment. Lest any hurt it, I will keep it night and day." As the sun is full of light, and the ocean of drops, so He is the full-stored treasury of needful grace. He is the tree laden with all fruits at all seasons. Whenever we approach, the produce is ripe, and bending low to the hand of faith. In Him are supplies of living grace for a living hour, of working grace for a working hour, of striving grace for a striving hour, of praying grace for a praying hour, of suffering grace for a suffering hour, of dying grace for a dying hour: grace for prosperity and for adversity—grace for the family, the closet, the sanctuary, and the public haunts of men—grace for the palace, the hut, the camp, the fleet—for those who rule, and for those who serve—grace for childhood, for manhood, and for age—grace for health, for sickness, and for pain—grace for those, who joy with the joyous, and for those, who mourn with the mourners, and weep at the grave. When the Father gave Jehovah-jireh to the Church, the gift was all things. "He that spared not his own Son, but delivered Him up for us all, how shall He not with Him also freely give us all things."

Reader, let me solemnly ask, have you sought Jehovah-jireh? Is Jesus the king and mainspring of your heart? Then know your rich possession. Joy in it. Live on it. Cease to spend money for that which satisfieth not. But eat the good, which is before you, and let your soul delight itself in fatness. Pine not in your own hut of penury, while His palace of all plenteousness courts your entrance. Lean not on your own crumbling staff, while the Rock of ages is near to uphold you.

It may be that some poor sinner hears of this all-sufficiency, and wails, Oh that I had interest in these blessed provisions! But alas! I starve, while others feast. Friend, why is it so? Why are you a stranger to this fertile mount? It is not, because Jehovah-jireh is far distant. It is not, because repelling barriers drive back. Scripture ever points to it, crying, "Yet there is room." Nay, Jesus draws near to the very door of your heart and knocks. In the lines before you, He beseeches you, Open unto Me, open unto Me. Will you tarry? Will you refuse? What! will you be poor now, and poor for ever —miserable now, and miserable for ever—while Jehovah-jireh, with inviting fulness, presents to you the overflowings of present grace, and future glory?

THE LADDER

"He dreamed, and behold a Ladder set up on the earth, and the top of it reached to heaven."
—GEN. xxviii. 12.

THE voice which cannot err, denounces, "Be sure your sin will find you out." Thus, by eternal law, misery stalks in transgressor's rear. Out of the Gospel-path our feet are in furrows sown with woe. Godliness is a quiet haven. Departure from it is a sea of trouble.

This truth is darkly written on many a sigh and many a tear. The case of Jacob painfully attests it. Behold him a downcast and a lonely wanderer. He treads a cheerless, solitary way. A journey is before him—long and perilous. He tenderly sorrows for delights behind him. He tremblingly forebodes the evils of to-morrow. But his keenest anguish is an upbraiding conscience. He leaves his home, because he first left his God.

O my soul, bear all things, suffer much, suffer long; but never venture, by ungodly schemes and ungodly guile, to run before the pillar and the cloud. The sin of man hastens not the set purposes of God. Nay, it rather stays the hand upraised to bless, and arms it with a chastening scourge.

Perhaps the declining sun never withdrew its light from one more deep in gloom than Jacob when he paused at Luz. The canopy of heaven was his only roof —the bare earth his couch—the rugged stone his pillow.

Instead of a tender mother's tender care, he had hardness in its hardest form.

But Jacob was an heir, from everlasting ages, of an everlasting portion, which is never lost. Hence an unchanging friend grieved in his every grief, and marked with sympathy his every step. The Lord, whose love is wisdom, and whose wisdom is love, leads His children into depths for their good; but leaves them not in depths to their hurt. It was so with Jacob. It will be so while saints on earth need to be brought low, that they may more securely rise.

Sleep closes his eyes. But in the night-watches marvellous teachings gladden the unclosed eye of faith. "Behold a Ladder set up on the earth, and the top of it reached to heaven." Here was no obscure sign of Him, who comforts most by revelations of Himself. The seed of the Woman, the Blessing of the Earth, the Covenant of His people is unfolded in clearer emblem. The Redeemer is displayed wondrous in His person, His work, His grace. Thus the patriarch found, as many find, that the absence of man is the nearness of God, and that the dark pages of trial are inscribed with new lessons of love. He arises, and exclaims, "Surely the Lord is in this place, and I knew it not."

Reader, this image, so radiant in Gospel-truth, vanished not when morning came. It has a power to teach in every age, and to make each lonely spot a Bethel to the pilgrim's heart.

Ponder well this Ladder. The like to it earth never saw. Mark its extent. It unites the worlds of Deity and man. It connects our sin-vile hovels with the abode of the Eternal. Resting on the ground, which our feet defile, it rises and stretches upward, and pierces the skies, and mounts to the very throne of God.

As such it pictures Him, who is at once the Highest of the high, and the Lowliest of the lowly—who, while he thinks it no robbery to be Jehovah's fellow, counts it all joy to be the poor man's kinsman. It shows Jesus, in the miracle of His person;—man, without ceasing to be God—God, without scorning to be man.

These are blessed tidings! Hold them fast, as the anchor of all hope—hold them up, as the beacon of all salvation—hold them forth, as realities of grandest moment. Our Jesus is the mighty God. All that there is in the Godhead of power, and might, and wisdom, and love, and dominion has been His, and must be His for ever. Eternity is His birth-place. Heaven is His home. His strength is Omnipotence. His arm is Infinity. His eye is All-seeing. His ear is All-hearing. His mind is Omniscience. He wills, and it is done. He puts on glory for a crown; and the brightness of that diadem is the redemption of souls. Think for ever, and you reach not the threshold of His vastness. Adore for ever, and you touch not the skirts of His praises. The summit of this Ladder is Jesus reigning, the ever living God.

Observe, too, that a Saviour less than this, could have been no Saviour for a sin-stained soul. For what is sin? It is an infinite evil, because it outrages every infinite attribute of God. Hence, it is inseparably linked with infinite woe.

Oh! who can tell the boundlessness of its dread results. It scales the heavens, and awakens wrath. It goes down to hell, and kindles unextinguishable flames. It rolls on, a ceaseless tide, throughout eternity. A moment did it. But no ages can undo. Who then can bear it away? The touch of man makes it more sinful. Angels' efforts are as a straw before a rock. But Jesus comes. His blood is sprinkled, and it vanishes. He hurls it from Him, and it is no more found. Why? Because Jesus is God. If the height of heaven were the pulpit; if the pealing thunder were the voice; if the universe were the audience: no more worthy utterance could sound, than that the blood of Jesus blots out sin, because the blood of Jesus is the blood of God.

Hence the delights, which Jesus gives to the awakened heart. It is conscious of iniquities towering to the skies. But, in the merits of a Saviour-God, a grave is found to bury all. Hence, too, we learn, why many think so little of this great salvation, and are content with a mock shelter of their own construction. They are dead as to what sin is. But when the Spirit once strikes the conscience with its sin-discovering rod, there can be no peace but in a devine refuge, no rest but under infinite covert. Christ, and Christ only, is such refuge, and such covert.

I fear, that to many this is a hidden truth. If once men saw it, they might dare to sport with the lightning, or to wrestle with the whirlwind; but they would not dare to trample on a Saviour-God.

This image proclaims Jesus, as invested also with our nature. The Ladder set up on the earth, is Jesus very man, as truly as He is very God. Yes, our Creator is our brother, that He may redeem us. Man must die. Jesus hangs on the cross—man, that He may represent —God, that He may suffice. His Deity enables. His manhood qualifies. The one is all-sufficiency. The other is all-fitness. Thus He cancels every debt, and makes all payment, and endures all punishment, and exhausts the whole curse, and works a glorious righteousness, and rescues all His sheep from the jaws of hell, and exalts His spouse in spotless lustre to the throne of His glory.

Next, the common uses of the Ladder instruct much in the divine art of using Jesus for hourly help. By the Ladder we leave the lower ground. By it we rise to things which are above. Just so, by Jesus there is open passage for our souls and services from our lowest estate to Zion's goodly heights. Sin not only left us prostrate, with no means to soar: but it fixed an intervening gulf, which unaided man could never pass. But Jesus interposes, and distance disappears.

Believer, your heart's desire is, that your prayers and praises may speak to God. Place them on Jesus, and they fly aloft. None can check their ascending speed. They are breathed below, and instantly resound on high. You long that your tears of penitence and sighs of shame may be heeded, where mercy reigns. There is no hindrance. Mourn with godly sorrow, clinging unto Jesus, and you melt a heavenly Father's heart. You strive in word and work to glorify His name. Labour with every effort intermixed with Jesus, and nothing can be done in vain. How sweet is it to the eye of faith, to see its every cry, and hope, and deed, thus carried buoyant to the court of God! Soon you must die. Be it so. Commit your departing spirit to the care of Jesus, and, released from its cage of clay, it will mount with eaglewings, and tarry not until the portals of eternal day are passed.

But the Ladder also affords means of descent. We need supplies from above. Through what channel can they come? Jesus alone presents an open course. Through Him the Spirit is outpoured. The light which dispels our darkness,—all views of saving love,—strength to begin and prosecute the heavenward race,—the joys, which make this wilderness to blossom as the rose, all wing their downward flight by this connecting line. The believer stands upon this Ladder, and voices run along it, each assuring him that his iniquities are pardoned, his person accepted, his soul saved. By this path the promises come down into his willing hand, and answers tell him that his prayers are heard. By this way ministering angels haste to encamp around, and to beat back the host of unseen foes. O my soul, can you enough bless Jesus, who thus unites a blessed people with a blessing God?

Reader, this subject is personal and practical. Tell me, then, have you found, do you duly prize, do you daily use these heaven-wrought steps? The solemn purport of the solemn question is this—Have you by faith grasped Jesus? Are you by faith cleaving unto Him? Faith is the eye which sees the Ladder;—the hand, which touches it;—the strength which holds it;—the feet which mount it. Has the Holy Spirit opened to you this figure, which was new life to Jacob? There is a ready test. Is the world beneath your tread? Do you trample on its love—fashions—maxims—principles? Feet set on a Ladder, no more rest on earth. The man, who is in Christ is high above the world. "Ye are not of the world, even as I am not of the world."

There is another test. Is yours an ascending life? On

the ladder there is upward movement. So the believer rises, step by step, from grace to grace. As there is no progress while one foot cleaves to the dust, so there is no growth in grace while lingering affections adhere to mire. We must be wholly Christ's or none of His.

Again, are your days all effort? There is no mounting without toil. Saints strain every nerve. They run an unwearied race. They wrestle in prayer. Their praises are as the ceaseless rapture of angelic chords. Their zeal flows, as the ocean's tide. They rest not digging in the mine of Truth, and scattering abroad the riches which they find. Thus they take heaven by holy violence. Reader, if you are some lazy loiterer, some dreaming slumberer, I tremble for you. Christ worked on earth. Christ works above. As is the Head, so are the members. As is the Lord, so are the servants.

Take heed, too, of false ladders. Satan has forged many. Their form is specious. Their height seems heaven-high. But the summit points hell-ward. The steps are rottenness, and soon they break. Salvation's Ladder is only one—Christ Jesus.

Believer, you profess to be on this Ladder. Hold fast. Watch and pray. Some, who seemed to climb well, have foully fallen. The most perilous slip is from the highest round. Perhaps you are conscious, that your foot has slipped. If so, arise and adore God, that you live. Arise and pray for grace, that you may re-ascend.

Unbeliever, you know nothing of this approach to God. You are afar off now. How will you bear to be far off for ever? Hear then; and may the Spirit bless the concluding word! There is a Ladder from every sin and every sorrow upon earth. But there is no ladder of escape from hell's wages, and from hell's pains. There are no stairs, by which the rich man may soar to Abraham's bosom. There is no up-let by which Judas can leave "his own place."

PENIEL

"Jacob called the name of the place Peniel."—GEN. xxxii. 30.

THE happiest heart in the world is that, in which faith and prayer have undisturbed rule. The truth of this statement follows from the fact, that faith has the key of heaven; and prayer has the ear of God. And who is happy as the man who is always free to enter within the veil, and hold communion there?

Reader, you would fain be happy among the happiest. —Beseech the Spirit, then, to fan these graces into brightest flame. With this desire let us hasten to Peniel —the scene of their liveliest exercise: and may we tarry there, until the holy fire kindle!

Jacob's hard servitude is ended. Home, with its fond endearments, is again before him. But, when he reaches the borders of his native land, he finds it garrisoned with perils. Esau, terrible in fury, mighty in force, is armed to intercept, and to destroy. The wanderer, who fled from death, returns to die.

But many terrors quench not faith. Jacob, urged by its impulse, flies directly to the mercy-seat. He humbles himself, as unworthy of grace's least crumb. Thus faith strips itself of all, that all the glory may be God's. He pleads that he is in obedience's path. Faith has no other ground on which to stand. He meekly claims the promises; for gracious promises are the title-deeds of hope.

But faith, busy in heaven, is not idle upon earth. In thoughtfulness and diligence it sows the seed, from which successes spring. With upward eye it labours and prevails; while unbelief looks inward—downward—and so fails.

The plans of Jacob are all wisely formed. Then darkness mantles the earth. But it brings no pillow for his head. He stands, and stands alone, on Jabbok's banks. We here see again, how grace gains oil for his lamp.

Reader, be sure of this, he is not a thriving and a well-stored saint, who is not much in solitary intercourse with God. No public ordinances, no social worship, no Christian fellowship, no mutual interchange of godly thought, can be a substitute for calm approach. It is when all things else are banished, that the smiles of Jesus are most sweet, His voice most clear, His comforts most supporting. Then the Word reveals its treasures, and the promises teem with life.

Many mourn lifelessness of spirit, and fruitlessness in work. The withering cause may be, that busy haunts are too busily frequented, and the quiet chamber is too rarely sought.

But is the lonely Jacob long alone? Oh no. A stranger suddenly draws near, and grapples with him, and strives with mighty energy to stay his progress, and to lay him in the dust. But who thus wrestles in the solemn stillness of this solemn night? The form is human, but the person is Divine. We read, " As a prince thou has power with God;" therefore the wrestler is God. Jacob confirms the fact: " I have seen God face to face." Thus, through the

veil of seeming mortality, we trace the angel of the everlasting covenant, our great Emmanuel, God manifest in
the flesh. As man, He spake with Adam in the garden;
as man, He walked by Abraham's side; as man, He here
struggles with the wandering patriarch. It is indeed a
rich display of grace, that Jesus thus should stand in
sinners' likeness on this sin-rank soil. But it is grace
above grace, that, in the fulness of time, He should take
our manhood into God, and wear it on the cross, and in
the grave: and then bear it to heaven, as His triumphal
robe for ever.

But wherefore is this wrestling? Every act of Jesus is
a volume written within and without in golden letters of
instruction. Thus Jacob, and every successive pilgrim,
learns, that the land of promise is only gained by battling
through opposing hosts. At the Lord's word, troops of
trials, and sorrows, and fears, and troubles arrange themselves against us. They strive, with determined might,
to stop our onward march. Behold Joseph. It was to
him no easy task to escape entangling foes. Consider Job,
and David, and Paul, and the Apostles, and all the
worthies, who shine in Scripture-page. What struggles,
what perils of overthrow were theirs! They wrestled
earnestly, and almost unto blood.

Reader, if you know little of spiritual conflict, it may
be you know nothing of the camp of Christ. Examine
yourself. Are you truly in the faith? If so, at the cross
you have drawn a sword, which never finds a scabbard
upon earth, and rarely finds a respite of repose. They,
who win the crown, fight a good fight. "The kingdom
of heaven suffereth violence, and the violent take it by
force."

But perhaps the struggle, thus severe, was short? Not so. It lasted until "the breaking of the day." Earth is a vale of darkness and of gloom. But yet a little while the shadows will flee away. The brightness of a cloudless eternity will dawn. The weary pilgrim will enter the city which has "no need of the sun, neither of the moon to shine in it, for the glory of God did lighten it, and the Lamb is the light thereof." Then, in a perfect place, there will be perfect rest.

Next the prowess of Jacob claims our wonder. Though nothing but a feeble worm, he is not crushed. He meets power with power, might with might, strength with strength, skill with skill. He will not—he cannot yield. He awakens again and again his energies. He exerts again and again every vigour of every nerve. He is but flesh and blood, as we are, yet he cannot be subdued.

It is all-important, that we rightly see what was the grand mainspring of Jacob's indomitable heroism. It cannot be too plainly urged, that it was faith. He was followed the Lord fully. He knew that the voice, which called him, was victory. Hence he was confident, that it were easier to scale and storm the heavens, than to frustrate his assured success. Faith is a rock, when thus based on the rock of promise. It is not of earth, therefore it is imperishable. It is of heaven, therefore its energies are Divine. It looks to Jesus, therefore it overlooks all difficulties. It leans on Jesus, therefore it is as firm as God.

But Jacob wrestled not in faith only, but in supplication and in tears. Thus Hosea writes—Hos. xii. 4, and Hosea's pen was in the hand of God. We hence learn, that faith is always in earnest, therefore it prays. It is always humble, therefore it weeps.

Here, again, a door is opened in heaven; and we see Jehovah vanquished by a praying saint. True prayer is indeed bold. It draws near to God, and closes with Him, and gives Him no rest, until an approving smile testifies that the suit is granted. God neither can, nor will, release Himself from the intensity of his efforts. He cannot, because the truth is set up in heaven, that prayer shall prosper. He will not, because prayer is the moving of His Spirit in the heart, and the speaking of His Spirit on the lips. To deny prayer would be to deny Himself. To be silent to it would be to be silent unto Himself. "If we ask anything according to His will, He heareth us: and if we know that He heareth us, whatsoever we ask, we know that we have the petitions that we desired of Him."

O my soul, examine well the Scripture's picture of prayer. It is "to take hold" of Him, Isa. lxiv. 7. It is "taking hold of His strength," Isa. xxvii. 5. It is to "give Him no rest," Isa. lxii. 7. Learn these truths in their power. Use them as the habit of your life. Then you will know prosperity and peace of soul.

But the heart strong in faith and prayer loses all nature's hardness. It becomes soft, as the sympathy of Jesus: and tender, as the whispers of His grace. Thus Jacob's streaming eye proclaimed, with what subdued sincerity he loved the Lord, whom he so tightly grasped —and how deeply he was melted by inward consciousness of sin's demerit.

Reader, remember, except you have faith, and prayer, and brokenness of heart, you have no signs of life. Prove, then, yourself at Peniel. Never quit it, until you hear these voices, "Great is thy faith, be it unto thee even as thou wilt." And again, "Behold he prayeth." And again, "She hath washed my feet with tears; therefore, her sins, which are many, are forgiven, for she loved much."

But we are so framed, that spiritual greatness may be a snare. It may unduly exalt, and lead us unduly to exult. That is destructive victory, which leaves the victor in the chains of pride. Our guardian Lord knew this, and since it is better to prevent than to heal, He "touched the hollow of Jacob's thigh, and it was out of joint." Here we have a mirror, which reflects many of the Lord's dealings with His favoured children. In prevailing they are crippled, lest by prevailing they should perish. Strong grace is checked by enfeebled flesh, lest it should climb the dizzy heights of self-esteem. Many halting infirmities convince them that a yielding Lord has power to lay low. They learn that prevalence is His gift, and not the wages of their might. They feel that they are broken reeds, except God works with them to will and to do.

Let us behold once more the triumphs of persevering faith. The angel concedes the victory, and sues to be released from the unyielding arms. Jacob, with limb disjointed, but with faith confirmed, seeks no advantage but an increase of heavenly favour. With holy boldness he exclaims, "I will not let Thee go, except Thou bless me." He cares not for healing of body, or for outward prosperity, he only asks for increased tokens of God's love, and for increased health within. "Bless me," is his prayer. Such noble yearnings are the Lord's delight. He honours them, because they honour Him. He crowns them with all that God Himself can give.

Count, if you can, the spoil which Jacob won, when the Lord blessed him there!

And now, a new name shall give perpetual fame to this exploit. Heroic deeds have endless life. Wherever the Word of God is preached or read, Israel is a title, which tells of Jacob's princely power with God and men. The record is true. As a prince, he constrained God to bless him. As a prince, he drew the heart of Esau like a captive into his arms.

Reader, be an Israelite indeed, and heaven is yours, and earth is yours. Heaven is yours to bless you. Earth is yours to serve you.

Jacob receives a name, and gives a name. He calls the place Peniel, "for I have seen God face to face, and my life is preserved."

Again I say, be an Israelite indeed, and every place will be your Peniel. In every scene you will behold God near. Through life, in death, you will have an eye to gaze undazzled on Him. Your secret chamber will be Peniel—as you kneel, God will come down, and shew His smiling face. The family-sanctuary will be Peniel— you will see Him extending the wings of mercy over you and yours. Every page of the Bible will be Peniel— bright with the radiance of Him, who is "the Light of Life," and "the Sun of Righteousness." Your post of daily toil will be Peniel; for you will set the Lord always before you. His earthly temples will be Peniel—in the prayers and praises of the assembled worshippers, in the proclamations of His truth, He will manifest Himself unto you, as He doth not unto the world. Your dying bed will still be Peniel. Jesus will come again, to bear you safely to a Father's home. Eternity will be a glorious

Peniel,—for it will be one unclouded view of God face to face.

Lord God of Israel, nothing is too hard for Thy power, nothing is too good for Thy love. Wilt Thou vouchsafe, by these poor lines, to bring some soul to Peniel!

NUMBERED WITH THE TRANSGRESSORS

" He was there in the Prison."—GEN. xxxix. 20.

A PRISON is a place of humiliation and of shame.
It is peopled by those who are under accusation of
crime, or who are awaiting the sentence of outraged law.
As such, the very name suggests ideas of infamy, and
chains, and death. The inmates are the actual or suspected perpetrators of evil, whose name is a reproach:
whom society casts out: who are as the noxious weed,
which must be rooted from the soil, and as the plague-
spot, which it is peril to approach.

But who is the prisoner, into whose cell these words
admit us? Within these walls of guilt we find a guiltless
man. The blameless Joseph is here immured. Without
offence, he is wronged as an offender—without transgression, he is numbered with transgressors.

Reader, the pure delight, the sanctifying feast of Scripture, consists in this. In every page the voice of Jesus
is heard—at almost every turn the image of Jesus is discerned. It is clearly so in the dungeon-scene before us.
Joseph in custody, reviled for uniquity which he knew
not, foreshadows Jesus, who, without sin, is made sin for
us. Yes, He for whom the heaven of heavens is no worthy
throne, is clothed for us in prison-garb, and tastes for us
the prison-shame. Hence the Spirit records, "He was
taken from prison and from judgment."

In approaching this truth, it is well to ask the amazing question, By whom was Jesus arrested? and often to ponder the more amazing reply. He was arrested by the justice of God. But wherefore? Had any fault stained His path? The bare thought is chilling, as the shock of blasphemy. Let it be met with a shudder of denial. Holiness was the essence of His being—the pulse of His soul. He was born the Holy Child Jesus. He lived the Holy Man Jesus. He died the Holy Sufferer. He rose the Holy Conqueror. He ascended in Holy triumph. Holiness is the sceptre of His kingdom for ever.

How, then, could Justice touch Him with a jailor's grasp? Because, though no shade of sin was in Him, still mountains of sins were upon Him. Although infinitely far from personal offence, He stood before God laden with all the countless transgressions of a countless multitude. Here is the godlike grace of God. He consents to remove guilt from the guilty, and to place it on the guiltless. He transfers the sins of the sinful to His sinless Son. Wondrous is the word, but true as wondrous, "The Lord hath laid on Him the iniquities of us all." So Jesus is our sin-bearing surety. He appears, by substitution, as covered, defiled, deformed by the whole accumulated mass of all our guilt. He is verily accounted, and is verily treated, as the perpetrator of every evil deed—as the speaker of every evil word—as the harbourer of every evil thought, which had stained, or should stain, each child in the redeemed family. Hence we understand the agony of His heart: Mine iniquities have taken hold upon Me, they are more than the hairs of my head. He presents His back to receive the hateful load. Justice finds it on Him. And therefore justly claims Him as his prisoner.

O my soul, have you by faith an interest in Christ? Then know your full relief. He snaps the chain, which would have dragged you down to hell. He passes under the dark waters of your pollution, that you may be reckoned clear of every stain. He becomes your unrighteousness, that you may be the righteousness of God in Him.

The Bible is a sealed book—the story of the cross is a beclouded page—peace is a delight untasted—hope is an idle fiction, until Jesus is prized as a substitute and a surety. How great the change, when He is so revealed! Then Justice shines in all its glory—Grace in all its brightness—Mercy in all its triumphs—Salvation in all its riches. Then the Gospel-trumpet sounds with power, "Behold the Lamb of God, which taketh away the sin of the world."

But in the Egyptian dungeon we see more than a resemblance of the blameless Jesus bearing blame. Transactions are transacted there, which help to unclasp the records of the empire of grace.

There are two offenders of no common note by Joseph's side. Human judgment looks in vain for difference between them. They are similar in outward calling—involved in like displeasure and degradation—expecting like ignominious end. But soon they are parted. One mounts the path of favour, and is crowned with honours—the other is left in bonds to die.

Such is the relation. But in it there is a predictive picture. It is a signal of the distant wonders of the cross. When man's rage and Satan's craft seem to prevail, and Jesus is led as a lamb to the slaughter, a corresponding circumstance occurs. To fill the cup of insult to the brim, notorious culprits are linked as His fit companions. But this studied effort to degrade Him to the level of the vilest sons of infamy, only attests His truth. The word which cannot fail, had said, " He was numbered with the transgressors." Behold the fulfilment. He is uplifted between two malefactors. When will vain men learn, that opposing rage only works out the purposes of God? The wildest rebellion is yoked to the chariot of His counsels, and His will. But let us draw nearer and trace the coinciding features of the two events. We take our station at Calvary. The accursed trees are upraised. The three are transfixed thereon. Jesus hangs in the midst.

Reader, again and again I beseech you, be often at this spot. That cross is the price of countless souls: the ransom of all the redeemed: and the glory of God in the highest. He knows nothing of sin's remission, who makes not these wounds his covert. He will never taste life, who washes not in the fountain here opened. He only enters heaven, who pleads this plea. Jesus here suffers, that He may wrest the sceptre from the hands of Satan,—overthrow the empire of darkness, and cause every perfection of Jehovah to be a pledge for salvation. It is a truth to be maintained before all the world, that the religion which glories not in the blood of the Lamb, is but a superstition of ignorance and conceit. The blood-besprinkled hope alone can live.

We look next to those, who writhe in torture on each side. It seems that they both begin to die, hard as the very nails which pierced them. Matt. xxvii. 44. Mark xv. 32. But soon a change—great as light from darkness

—life from death—love from hate, passes over the one.
He loathes the sin which once he fondled. He confesses
its enormous malignity, and he professes to fear the God
whom he had scorned. But whence this newness of every
feeling? It is not the fruit of outward circumstance.
All visible appearances are common to them both. But
one alone is touched, and taught, and enlightened, and
turned. How is he thus softened? Some invisible power
has entered the recesses of his heart, and there crushed
every godless foe. It can only be the Spirit of the Most
High. It is His sole prerogative to convince of sin.
Without Him the outward fact of trial, affliction, pain,
suffering, warning, threat, entreaty, never opens the
blinded eye, or turns the wandering feet. Whenever
awakened conscience cries, Behold I am vile, I loathe
and abhor myself, Omnipotence has aimed the blow,
which brought the rebel to his knees.

But more than this. A trusting eye now gazes upon
Jesus. To the mocking mob He seems "a very worm
and no man"—but through all the rags and poverty of
humanity, through all the disguise of blood and of infamy, faith knows the King of kings, the Conqueror of
Satan, the divine Deliverer, the all-subduing Saviour.
The shameful cross is discerned as the glorious high
throne of incarnate Deity. Here again we see the mighty
Spirit's work. He alone can show Jesus to the soul. But
when He speaks the word, the despised and rejected of
men is loved and adored as the chief among ten thousand,
the altogether lovely, the one dispenser of the mercies
of salvation.

But this is not all. A man may confess, I have sinned,
and yet perish. Such was the case of Judas. The know-

ledge of the head may boast, " We know Thee, who Thou art," and never obtain life. Such is the case of devils. To gain interest in Christ, there must be a personal application to Him—close dealing with Him. But when the soul is deeply taught its need, and sees that Christ alone can minister relief, it cannot be kept back. It receives a strength, which bursts all fetters—wades through oceans of difficulty—surmounts mountains of obstacles—and never rests, until, safe in His sheltering arms, it hears the welcome of His lips. It was so with the dying thief. Mark his cry, " Lord, remember me." I am perishing, but Thou canst save me. The flames of hell almost encompass me, but Thou canst rescue. " Lord, remember me."

Reader, is your need less than his? No. For it is great as need can be. And things infinite admit not of comparison. Is your loss less precious than his? Is your eternity less eternal? It cannot be. Have you, then, cried with his intensity, " Lord, remember me?" Happy they, whose hearts thus wrestle with the Lord! They win the priceless prize of heaven. They gain the matchless gain of everlasting joy. It was so with the dying thief. So it will always be. Quick is the heart of Christ to feel, and swift His word to cheer. " This day thou shalt be with Me in Paradise." There is no doubt, no demur, no delay. A sinner mourns, the Saviour pities. A sinner looks, the Saviour smiles. A sinner speaks, the Saviour hears. A sinner prays, the Saviour answers. The petition is, " Remember." The grant is " Thou shalt be with Me." Blessed sorrow! blessed faith! blessed prayer! blessed grace! blessed Saviour! Thou art worthy to be called Jesus. Thou art worthy to reign on

the throne of the adoring heart. Thou are worthy to be
extolled with every breath. Thou are worthy to be proclaimed by every lip in every clime, in every age. Thou
are worthy to be the eternal hymn of eternal hallelujahs.

It may be, that I address some, who, through many
years of worldly-mindedness, and unbelief, have been
tottering on the precipice of perdition. But you yet live;
and Christ still lives; and the Spirit has ever a heart of
tenderness, and an arm of power. Therefore there is
hope. The door, though closing, is not yet closed. The
thief pressed forward and found grace. He had a golden
moment; he seized it, and he is now with Jesus. What
will you do? Will you sit still and perish?

But perhaps Satan, that liar from the beginning, is
suggesting the thought, that a death-bed will bring grace
to repent, and to believe, and to seek mercy. Believe
him not. Was it so with the other thief? The gnawing
of agony only hardened him. Hell was near, but he
neither saw, nor feared, nor shunned it. And now from
the midst of a fiery lake he warns, as a frightful beacon,
that death approaching with sure tread, and touching
with strong hand, neither changes the heart, nor begets
faith.

But let me rather hope, that you have drunk truly of
the cup of life. If so, you differ, you widely differ,
you infinitely differ from former self, and from the mass
around. But whence the difference? Surely you will
gratefully allow, Sovereign love looked lovingly on
me—conquering grace dealt graciously with me. Surely
you will add, By the power of sin I was what I was.
By the grace of God I am what I am. Sin numbered

me with transgressors. But eternal purpose and
eternal love laid help for me on One that is mighty.
Jesus was numbered with the transgressors, that I
might be numbered with His saints in glory everlasting.

THE STORE-HOUSES OPENED

"Joseph opened all the store-houses."—GEN. xli. 56.

HE has much to learn, who has not found a garland of delights in Joseph's story. The variety of incident, the rapidly changing scene, the crowded picture of man in every character and every circumstance, make it a choice pleasure-ground for young and old, for peasant and for sage. The sacred pen, pointed by heaven, and deeply dipped in the human heart, enters each chamber, in which feeling dwells. We weep with the weeping father: we grieve in his protracted grief: we revive, when he lives again in his son restored. We tremble with the youth trembling in the pit. We sigh with him sighing in his exile. We take courage with him trampling on his temptation. We are disconsolate with him, disconsolate in his dungeon. We triumph with him, when he surmounts reproach, and takes his seat as the ruler of a mighty empire.

But the grand value of the narrative is not the simple style, the tender pathos, the amazing events, the winding thread of providential arrangement, or the happy end. These lead the mind through luxuriant fields of captivating interest. But if this be all, the profit is as a fading flower, or as a morning gleam. He only gains, who gains a blessing for his soul. The soul is the real man. All else is earthly as earth: and transient as time. The book, the employ, the companion, the scene, which adds not to spiritual store, whatever may be the seeming promise or the present attraction, is an injury, an enemy, a poison, and a blight.

The Scripture before us is precious, because every view of Joseph exhibits Jesus. Who is the envied, and hated, and rejected of his brethren? Who is the sold for pieces of silver; the cast out into Egypt; the numbered with the transgressors; the apparent culprit between two offenders, of whom one is exalted, the other perishes? Who is raised from the prison to the right hand of majesty? In all these outlines, is not Jesus seen? He it is on whose shoulder the government is laid. He it is, who rescues His kindred from perishing. He it is, whose heart yearned over them, when they knew Him not. He it is, to whom the perishing must flee. He it is, who has the key of all supplies. The name is Joseph. The true image is Jesus.

But the text of this chapter limits our view to one feature of this spacious picture. The plenty diffused by Joseph is the plenty which is in Jesus. Let us draw near, then, to this treasury of treasuries. And may the Spirit, sweet in His omnipotence, and omnipotent in His sweetness, open our eyes to see its fulness—and our hands to take of it!

The narrative discloses a universal misery. Affliction in an appalling form brooded over a prostrate world. The staff of life failed. Hunger presided grimly at every board. The pallid cheeks, the hollow voice, told the sad tale of death begun. But amid all the hopelessness there is hope. Store-houses had been filled with grain; and Joseph was appointed, as a minister of mercy, to deal out relief.

The glad tidings fly gladly through the land. Crowds throng the life-restoring gates. Do you ask, why is there speed in every step—and eagerness in every look? Want touches them with an iron grasp. Home gives no hope. In toil there is no help. One only can relieve. To linger is to die. To apply to Joseph is to regain abundance. They rush from ruin into remedy.

Here we see the starving sinner fleeing unto Jesus. There is a day, in which poor man sits careless in the hovel of his need—content with husks of his own procuring. But when light from on high reveals his impoverished state, then a very earthquake shakes the whole fabric of his delusion. He finds that, as a terrific famine, sin sucks his life-blood. In mercy's hour he hears, You yet may live. There is bread enough, and to spare, in Jesus. What now can keep him back? He bounds over all mountains of difficulty: he wades through all oceans of hindrance: he strides over all opposing taunts and sneers: he breaks every detaining fetter. You may tie the winds with a thread: you may allay the storm with a word: you may sweep back the ocean with a feather, but you cannot stay the awakened sinner, who hungers for a crumb of mercy, and who knows, that to reach Jesus is to have all-sufficiency for ever.

But perhaps I address some, who have not fled in rapid flight towards this one centre of relief. Awake, awake, ere yet you sleep the sleep of death. Do you not know, that your land is famine-stricken? It is so. Sin, as a desolating waste, has ravaged all the field of nature. It yields no healthful pastures for the soul. It has no regaling fruits with juice of life. It is only a rank wilderness of thorns, and briers, and noxious weeds. You must get heavenly manna, or you die. The hands of Jesus alone dispense it. Will you not, then, arise and seek Him?

Others, with some consciousness of peril, and some efforts to escape, yet pine and languish. They set forth in search of food. But Satan's false direction-posts mislead them. So they turn aside to granaries, which error has erected, and which self has furnished. Here they repast on the empty bubbles of outward rite, and forms, and unsubstantial show. The cravings of sense and imagination may be satisfied. But sense and imagination are not the soul.

Others advance farther, and yet never reach the coffers, in which saving treasure is laid up. It may be, they pause at the portals of God's word. This guide is indeed divine. In every word of every verse the voice from heaven speaks. But to listen to instruction is not safety. The knowledge of the repository is not food for the famishing. Ah! miserable woe, to fall into hell with Scripture on the lip!

Others rest in the Church as their sufficient aid. It is indeed a heaven-raised fabric. It is the pillar and ground of the truth. It warns and teaches. But it can neither give nor retain life. Ah! miserable woe, to drop into hell from the scaffold of salvation!

Others feed only on Sacraments. These are indeed ordained of God, as precious signs and seals of grace—but signs are not the substance, neither are seals the deeds. Ah! miserable woe, to enter hell with Sacramental elements in the hands!

Others are content with the refreshment, which faithful ministers afford. They are indeed the stewards of Christ's

mysteries, the heralds of His grace, the under-shepherds
of the flock. It is their province to go in and out before
the sheep. But the true nourishment of the soul is not
kept by them. Ah! miserable woe, to enter hell through
the schools of heaven!

Others delight themselves in labours for Christ's name.
Works are indeed the evidence of faith, and shoots from
its root. But the evidence is not the motive—the shoot
is not the root. Ah! miserable woe, to lie down in hell
in a garb of seeming godliness!

Reader, believe me, to obtain support, and grace, and
life, we must go directly unto Jesus. No hands but His
deal out supplies.

Does any tremblingly inquire, Will a ready welcome
meet my suit? Myriads have sought, and all have found.
He never yet sent suppliants away. The decree is sure:
" Him, that cometh to Me, I will in no wise cast out."
His character varies not: " He hath filled the hungry
with good things." The silver tone of the call yet
sounds; " Eat, O friends; drink, yea, drink abundantly,
O beloved."

Do you further ask, What are the provisions of this
banquet-house? I could more easily count ocean's sands,
than tell the plenteousness, which is here spread. " Hear,
O ye heavens, and give ear, O earth." The Lord gives
His body and His blood for food. " My flesh is meat
indeed, and my blood is drink indeed." Faith stretches
out an eager hand, and adoringly partakes. But how?
Not with carnal lip. The thought is heresy. Reason
scorns it. Infidelity derides it. Scripture denies it. All
experience rejects it as a pitiful and profitless conceit.
No. Faith takes and digests the feast with the pure and

holy relish of the heart. The hidden manna is the savoury truth of Christ's body given, and Christ's blood poured out for sin. The spiritual reception of this fact is strength, and vigour—not to a crumbling house of clay —but to a new-born, ever-living soul. The inner man thus nourished, fights, with a giant's might, the fight of faith, and mounts up with eagles' wings towards Zion's heights.

Here, too, we gain the full nourishment of precious promises and Scripture-truths. When the Lord's hand applies them, then every word is spirit and is life. The poor, the weary, and the heavy-laden come. Trials, afflictions, and temptations weigh them down. They crave support, and they find it in gracious testimonies, and refreshing tokens of eternal love. Like Jonathan, they taste the honey. Their eyes are lightened, and their spirits cheered.

Indeed, there is no sustenance for Christian life, which is not here provided. It is a grand word, " It pleased the Father that in Him should all fulness dwell." Fulness not for Himself, for He is glorious as God can be—but that He may replenish weary pilgrims. As the sun is light and gives light: so Jesus is grace, and diffuses grace. The one experience of all His suppliants is, " Of His fulness have all we received, and grace for grace." The empty return full. The impoverished are made rich: the weak become strong: the faint revive: the drooping are renewed in vigour: the famished are fed.

To some there was a tedious journey to the store-houses of Egypt. But the rapid flight of faith brings us in one moment to the depository of grace.

Perhaps there were appointed hours, at which Joseph

distributed the grain. These gates are widely open day and night.

Crowds might be detained, while others were relieved. Jesus is always waiting to give ready ear.

The Egyptian granaries, though very full, might be exhausted. Our supply is not in a cistern, but in an ever-flowing spring. The contents are deep as infinity, boundless as God.

The Egyptians are required to purchase. We receive all, without money, and without price. Over the Gospel-mart is inscribed, " Ask, and ye shall have."

Do you perish for need of the bread of life? Remember, you are unfed, because you will not feed: you starve, because you will not take.

Are you as a sapless plant with little fruit and scanty shoots? It is because you rarely seek the Joseph of the Gospel. But think again. " He giveth more grace." He is come, that you might have life, and that you might have it more abundantly.

Child of God, you have drawn near. You know how quickly to your cry the door flew open. You sued for pardon. It was granted. You sought for joy and peace. Your heart was filled. You told your need of light and guidance. Directing rays shone brightly on your path. A suppliant eye longed for some tokens of a Saviour's love. Soon you beheld his heart, engraven with your name,—bleeding for your ransom.

Now go and show your gratitude. You best can do this by constant coming to the Store-house door. Jesus ever stands to open. Will not you ever stand to knock? He lives a life to give. Will not you live a life to take and to dispense?

SHILOH

" Until Shiloh come."—GEN. xlix. 10.

SHILOH is a word first uttered in a dying chamber, and by dying lips.

Reader, how soon may your eyes be closing to the speck of earth, and opening on the expanse of boundless being! Accept the humble hope, that in such hour Shiloh, which is Christ, may be your solid stay: and that the light of His presence may make the dark vale bright.

Shiloh introduces us to a solemn scene, in which death and joy stand hand in hand. The aged patriarch had known the perils and tossings of a stormy voyage. But the longed-for haven now opens to receive him. Our billows, too, may rage and swell. But let us struggle on in hope. They waft the believer by rapid tide to the calm water of eternal rest.

Shiloh is almost the last testimony of the expiring parent. Happy is it thus to leave a legacy of cheering blessings to those, who watch around us! Happy to direct the mourner's thought to Him, who has abolished death, and who will gather all His children into one home of blessed union—where union is eternity.

Shiloh.—It is a sweet and mighty name. Sweet, for it is His, whose name is as ointment poured forth. Mighty, for it is His, whose name is above every name. In it He comes near to hold enlightening converse with our minds.

His love delights to reveal the riches of His goodness, and of His glory, to His people. Thus while the highest angels veil their faces while they worship at His throne, He draws the poor sinner to His side, and bids him read, line upon line, the records of His grace. He passes before us in a long train of titles: each giving fresh knowledge and awakening fresh rapture. But while other names shine each as one ray of attribute, Shiloh is a very wreath of light. Others are as separate jewels. This is a full-set diadem. It has many tongues. May each, by the Spirit's power, speak much to us!

Shiloh is the Sent. "Go, wash in the pool of Siloam, which is by interpretation, Sent." John ix. 7. Here then Jesus spreads, as it were, His credentials before us. He bids us mark, that He comes not without authority; that He is commissioned by some court. Yes, truly, He brings a message from a far-off kingdom. He speaks an absent Sovereign's will.

By whom is He thus sent? Hear one of the many voices, with which Scripture scatters the reply throughout its pages. "In this was manifested the love of God toward us; because that God sent His only-begotten Son into the world, that we might live through Him. Herein is love, not that we loved God, but that He loved us, and sent His Son to be the propitiation for our sins," 1 John iv. 9, 10. The eternal Father sends the eternal Son. We adore the love of Jesus, in visiting this earth. We adore the love of the Spirit, in aiding us to see His work and hear His voice. Let us adore, with every power of adoration, the love of the Father, in opening the door by which He came. The praise of every breath can never reach the glorious Giver's glorious gift. The fountain of redemption lies deep in the Father's heart. The first link of salvation's golden chain is in the Father's hand. The thought, Let us send a Saviour, sprang into being in His mind. " God so loved the world, that He gave His only begotten Son." "God commendeth His love toward us, in that, while we were yet sinners, Christ died for us." Let us strive to measure the greatness of the love in the greatness of the Sent. The Father's Shiloh is the Father's Son. In the fulness of time "God sent forth His Son." If He had emptied heaven of all its shining hosts, and despatched them in glorious array, it would indeed have been a brilliant embassage. But all would have been as dross, compared with Jesus. He as much transcends all multitudes of angels, as the Creator can transcend the thing, which He has made. He had lived a whole eternity, while they were wrapt in nothingness. How much more precious He than they!

Could then no other Shiloh execute the errand? Impossible. The work to be accomplished is the sinner's redemption. Infinite righteousness must be spread over the unrighteous. For this Jesus is needed. For this Jesus is sent. Expiation must be made for sins, infinite in number, and each infinite in guilt, and therefore Jesus comes. Jesus alone is able to atone.

Believer, read then in your Shiloh the tender graces of the Father's heart. He sends so much to save you, that He could send no more. Read the boundless worth of your soul. Shiloh's merits are its only price. Read the unutterable anguish of the lost. Shiloh alone had strength to bear it for you. Read the inconceivable glories of the redeemed. That heaven must be bright indeed, which is the purchase of a divine Shiloh's blood.

Shiloh.—The next expression of the word is—He for whom it is reserved: He to whom the kingdom appertains: He, who is the heir of all things. Thus Jesus is revealed, as seated on the throne of redemption's glories. We catch the sound of the proclamation, "There was given Him dominion, and glory, and a kingdom, that all people, nations, and languages should serve Him: His dominion is an everlasting dominion, which shall not pass away, and His kingdom, that which shall not be destroyed." Here is that sure purpose, and that sure promise, which is faith's high tower of undoubting confidence. Here is the foreshadow of the onward coming of victories, which must be. What though the world is mad, in mad rebellion against Shiloh? What though iniquity may seem a mighty potentate? What though the pure truths of Jesus are trodden as the mire beneath ungodly feet? The name of Shiloh laughs all foes to scorn. It is a banner of triumph, on which is inscribed, His is the kingdom, and the sceptre, and the sway: "Yet have I set my King upon my holy hill of Zion:" "Sit thou at my right hand, until I make Thine enemies Thy footstool:" Yet a little while, and Jesus will take to Himself His great power and reign, "and the wicked shall be silent in darkness."

Believer, cease then to be downcast, because you see not yet all things put under Him. Your Shiloh must prevail. Look back and see what wonders have followed the preaching of His name. Look around and see what numbers are flying to the cross, as doves to their windows. Look onward, and delight yourself in the view of fields ripening for the harvest. In following Him, you follow a mighty Conqueror to mighty victories. In His service you march to blessed triumphs. How soon, and every foe shall lick the dust! How soon, and every cry of opposition shall have died away! How soon, and His chariot-wheels shall drive gloriously, and Satan, and the grave, and hell, and all the legion of sin's slaves, shall writhe in captive chains! The kingdom is reserved for Shiloh. It may be you have often prayed, "Thy kingdom come." It is at hand. The answer tarries not. How will it find you? Does faith bear witness, that you are called to inherit the kingdom? Or does conscience tremble, lest His glory should be your everlasting shame. Prepare to meet Him. Shiloh's reign is at the door.

Shiloh brings another message. It means—His Son. Do you ask, whose Son? Faith takes the largest view. It answers, the Son of God—for Jacob's mind is fixed on God. The Son of Man—for Jacob speaks of Judah. Deity and humanity are here claimed for Christ, and both are His.

He is Jehovah's Son. This is the keystone of salvation's arch. This is the light of salvation's firmament. He is one with the Father. One in nature—one in essence—one in every perfection. In every sense He is His co-eternal and co-equal fellow. From everlasting to everlasting He is the Mighty God. Before all worlds, and world without end, He is God over all. They know no hope, who know not Christ, as God. It is mockery to say, "Look unto Me and be ye saved," unless the speaker be divine. If He were less, He could not remove one speck of iniquity from a sin-soiled soul. It cannot be too firmly maintained, that each sin is an infinite evil, and therefore requires the expiation of infinite merit. But you have all infinities in Shiloh. He is omnipotent to bear away the countless sins of the whole multitude of the redeemed. He is sufficient to clothe them with righteousness meet for heaven. He is irresistible to subdue every foe. He is all-glorious to present them all-glorious before the throne of God—and to encircle them with all glories for ever. This He can do, because He is Shiloh, the Son of God.

But Shiloh—His Son—may mean the Son of Judah. Here then we have another sign of the Woman's Seed. Jesus shall be the Lion of Judah's tribe. He shall put on the rags of our poor flesh, as the offspring of one of Judah's daughters—cradled in Judah's city. This is the wonder of heaven, of earth, of hell, of all eternity. Does it fill your heart with raptures of adoring praise? Do you find in it precious token of His boundless love, and sure proof that He is qualified to redeem?

Ponder well the fact. If Christ be not very man, there is no atoning death—no expiating blood—no justifying righteousness—no kindred sympathy—no open way to God—no centre of union. God is infinitely far from man. And man is immeasurably below God. But Shiloh comes to make them one, with every property and faculty of man, and every power of God. Faith is satisfied, and cries, My kinsman, my Lord, my God, my full, my complete Salvation!

But there is yet another chord from Shiloh's harp. It sounds the sound of Peacemaker. What sweet music to a poor trembling sinner! He knows, that sin makes tremendous enmity. It turns the heart of God to wrath. It fills his lips with threats, and His hands with destroying weapons. It builds the walls of hell, and kindles the fire, and hurries its victims to the never-dying worm.

But Shiloh flies to earth, and wrath departs, and love resumes the throne, and peace puts on the crown. He takes away the provoking cause. He buries sin in the fathomless ocean of His blood. God looks on the believer wrapt up in Jesus, and loves him with immeasurable love, and blesses him with countless blessings, and honours him with heaven's honours, and glorifies him with heaven's glories. Shiloh is our peace with God.

But He is more. He causes the waters of perfect peace to flow in sweetest tides over the troubled surface of an awakened soul. When the Spirit-taught conscience feels what we really are, and what we really merit, what agonies distract! There can be no ease, no hope, until Shiloh bear us to His cross, and open to us His wrath-appeasing wounds. But when we see all our punishment descending upon Him, each fear is lulled to rest. The storm of anguish becomes the calm of heaven's own joy. The trial of life, the apprehensions of trouble, the threats of poverty and of pain, the frowns of the ungodly, no more can harass. He, who has Shiloh in his heart, has no room for anything but peace. He hears no voice, but that of the Prince of Peace, always whispering, "Peace I leave with you, my peace I give unto you." Such is the Shiloh promised by the dying patriarch. He is come. He has fulfilled all.

Reader, put not aside this feeble testimony, until you can say, I know Him—I love Him—I cling to Him in all the offices, which the large terms reveal.

SALVATION

"I have waited for Thy Salvation, O Lord."—GEN.
xlix. 18.

SALVATION! Blessed be God, that our fallen earth
has heard the joyful sound! It is unheard in hell.
Reader, blessed be the grace, which brought it to your
ears! Multitudes of man's family are strangers to it.
But thrice-blessed be the Spirit's love, if it is the sweetest
melody which charms you—the loudest note, by day and
by night, of your unwearied praise! To multitudes, it
is a tuneless cymbal.

Salvation! It peoples the many mansions of the
heavenly kingdom. It is the bliss of the ever-blissful.
It is the joy of the ever-joyful. It is the happiness of the
ever-happy. It is the song of the ever-singing. It is the
peace of the ever-peaceful. It is the rest of the ever-rest-
ing. It is the glory of the ever-glorified. O my soul! see
to it, that you are saved.

Salvation! It is a roll written by Jehovah's pen. It is
the decree of Divine councils: the fruit of omniscient
mind: the first-born of unmeasured love: the perfection
of eternal thought: the strength of omnipotence. It is
the fabric, which every attribute of God erected, with
concurring hand; in which every stone is brought by
mercy, and shaped by wisdom, and laid by grace; in
which there is no defect—no blemish—no decay. It is

the soul-built temple, which will rise and shine in growing splendour through all ages. O my soul! see to it, that you are saved.

Salvation! It is the work for which Jesus was born in Bethlehem, and lived on earth, and died at Calvary, and descended into the grave, and burst the bonds of death, and mounted to heaven, and sits on the right hand of God. For this He trod the lowest vale of shame and grief. For this He drank the deepest cup of wrath and torment. For this He grappled with all the powers of darkness. For this He reigns and prays on high.

It is the work, for which the Spirit seeks our earth, and knocks at the barred entrance of the sinner's heart. For this He assails the fortress of self-love, and reveals the perils of sin, and wrestles with ignorance and vain excuses. For this He strives, until the arms of rebellion fall, and the contrite soul flees to the cross, and embraces Jesus, and shelters in the sure refuge of His wounds. O my soul! see to it, that you are saved.

Salvation! It is the first message, which mercy uttered to a ruined world. It is the end of every prophecy—the purport of every precept—the beauty of every promise— the truth of every sacrifice—the substance of every rite— the song of every inspired lip—the longing desire of every renewed heart—the beacon, which guides through the voyage of life—the haven, to which the tides of grace convey—the end of faith, the full light of hope, the home of love. O my soul! see to it, that you are saved.

Salvation! It is the absence of this blessing, which builds the prison-house of hell, which kindles the never-quenched fires—which forges the eternal chains—which wraps the dreary regions in one mantle of blackness—

which gives keenness to the undying worm—which blows up the smoke of torment—which gives the bitterness of despair to the hopeless wail. O my soul! see to it, that you are saved.

Better not have been born, unless you are saved. Life is a curse, death is the abyss of misery, without this joy. To what profit would it be, to hold the sceptre of kingdoms, to call the whole race of men our vassals, to look around on all the world as our own possession, to see in every creature only an instrument of our indulgence, to revel in every ease and luxury, to drink the fullest cup of pleasures, to sit on the highest throne of honour, to be caressed by all the affection, and to be extolled by all the adulation of man, unless you are saved? All these things, if they could be multiplied beyond our powers to calculate, and piled beyond our faculties to grasp, and stretched to time, which we could not count, would be as nothing, and less than nothing, would be only the mockery of splendid woe—without salvation. Gain this, and all, and more than all, is gained. Lose this, and no words can express, no thought conceive, the amount of wretchedness, which is the endless doom. O my soul! see to it, that you are saved.

Do you ask, but where is this treasure, so surpassing all treasures, to be found? It is all in Jesus Christ. He is full, and perfect, and eternal Salvation. Hear the voice from heaven: "Thou shalt call His name Jesus, for He shall save His people from their sins." Hear the lips which were touched by the living coal: "Believe on the Lord Jesus Christ, and thou shalt be saved." Hear the testimony of the Spirit: "This is a faithful saying, and worthy of all acceptation, that Christ Jesus came into the world to save sinners." Here is truth—unerring truth—divine truth—high as the heavens—clear as light —sure as God. Sophistry cannot perplex it. Falsehood cannot deny it. Salvation is Jesus Christ.

You may be clothed in purple and fine linen, and fare sumptuously every day, as Dives did—and not be saved. You may rule vast provinces, and command vast armies, as Pharaoh and Nebuchadnezzar did—and not be saved. You may be fair and lovely to behold, as Absalom was— and not be saved. You may belong to a Church, pure, and simple, and apostolic, and blessed with holy ordin- ances, as Ananias and Sapphira did—and not be saved. You may live under the highest blaze of Gospel-teaching, as Judas did: nay, you may bear witness to the truths of Jesus, as he did—and not be saved. You may be exalted unto heaven in privileges and opportunities, as Chorazin, Bethsaida, and Capernaum were—and not be saved. You may have the shrewdest intellect, as Ahithophel had— and not be saved. But you cannot believe in the Lord Jesus Christ, and fail of Salvation. The word abides for ever, "Whosoever believeth in Him should not perish, but have everlasting life." Let the rich man believe, and he is saved. Let the poor man believe, and he is saved. Let the young believe—let the old believe—let the wise believe—let the ignorant believe—and all is safe. Christ is theirs, and Christ is Salvation.

Does any eager soul exclaim, Tell me further, wherein Salvation's blessedness consist? Is it a blessed rescue, to change ceaseless wailings into endless praise: the black- ness of darkness into the glories of brightness beyond the sun in his strength: the woeful dungeons of the lost into the palace of Jehovah: the chains of misery into palms of triumph: the beds of flame into the throne of glory? Salvation effects this. Is it a glorious work, to turn hatred into love: cursing into adoration: every fiendish passion into one flow of holy peace: and to exalt the poor sinner from being the comrade of devils into partnership with the saints in light? Salvation speaks, and this is done.

Does any add, Let me clearly understand, how this is all accomplished? Come, see the excellent things, which Jesus works. He saves, by rescuing from hell. He saves, by giving title to heaven. He saves, by making meet for heaven.

All praise be to the Captain of our Salvation. He saves, by rescuing from hell. Hell is the home of sin:—the wages of sin. The steps of sin tend towards it. The toil of sin is to earn this payment. But if sin be removed, hell is escaped. Now Jesus takes away sin. From His wounded side, and pierced hands, from the cross on which He died, from the altar on which He makes atonement, a stream of blood flows forth, of efficacy so mighty —so cleansing—that it washes away every speck and stain of iniquity. Plunge all the sins of all, who ever sinned, into this unfathomable ocean of merit, and they disappear for ever. The foulest transgressor bathed in this blood of atonement becomes so pure, so white, that God can discern no blemish in him. Satan can no more allege a fault, or establish a claim against him. Why should he be made over to the dungeons of that jailor? He owes no debt, for all is discharged: he has no mark of perdition on his brow: for all is obliterated. How can he receive the wages of wrath? They have been already paid to the Surety in his stead. Thus Jesus saves His people from hell, because He breaks the only chain, by which the sinner can be tied down. No sin, no wrath—no sin, no hell. But sin can no more be found when Jesus casts it from view, far as the east is from the west.

He saves, by giving title to heaven. He not only expiates on the cross. But moreover, He weaves, by His most pure and Godlike life on earth, a mantle of divine righteousness. This completely clothes all who are one with Him. His fulfilment of the law is reckoned their very doing. Thus robed in celestial robes, the redeemed have right to pass the gates of life. They are free to the citizenship of heaven. They are privileged to advance to the very throne of God. No seat is too high, no honours too vast for those, who shine in this garment of Salvation.

But the believer needs more than a key to unlock the heavenly gates. He must bring more than outward decoration. There must be an inward fitness, or joy would not be joy. There must be a nature congenial to the nature, which prevails. The atmosphere above is all holiness. There is but the one pulse of perfect love in that abode. To an unrighteous man, this home would be a dismal solitude. From every sight he would shrink, every sound would be a discordant note. The presence of the godly inmates would be reproach and misery. Their one employ would be hateful irksomeness. Their one song, " Holy, Holy, Holy, Lord God of Hosts," would fill him with vexation and distress. But the Salvation of Jesus prepares for such rapture. He by His Spirit dethrones the love of sin: implants delight in God: takes barren hardness out of the soil: fills it with the flowers of Paradise: transforms it into the garden of the Lord. He of God is made unto us sanctification, as well as re-

demption. His pure robe decks those only, whom His
spirit purifies. It is the hand of a new nature, which receives the new raiment. "The king's daughter is all
glorious within," as well as arrayed in "wrought gold."
All, who present the plea of Christ's righteousness, exhibit conformity to His likeness, and bring heart-longings
for His immediate presence. Such is the great Salvation. O my soul! see to it, that you are saved.

It is great, because willed, provided, accepted by a
great God, even the Father: because wrought out and
finished by a great God, even Jesus: because applied by
a great God, even the Spirit. It is great, because it averts
great woe: bestows great grace: and blesses a great multitude. O my soul! see to it, that you are saved.

Happy is life, when we can say with Paul, "He hath
saved us, and called us with an holy calling." Happy is
prayer, when the Spirit supplies the loud Amen. "Whosoever shall call upon the name of the Lord shall be
saved." Happy is praise, when faith adds the chorus,
"The Lord Jehovah is my strength and my song, He
also is become my Salvation." Happy is death, when
truth can testify, as in Jacob's case, "I have waited for
Thy Salvation, O Lord." Happy is eternity, when adoration sings, "Salvation to our God, which sitteth upon the
throne, and unto the Lamb."

O my soul! see to it, that you are saved.

But give ear, the Spirit warns, "How shall we escape,
if we neglect so great Salvation?"

SOME OTHER
BANNER OF TRUTH
TITLES

THE LIFE OF JOSEPH

George Lawson

The story of Joseph is one of the most intriguing and attractive of all biblical narratives. Its importance is underlined by the fact that approximately one quarter of the Book of Genesis is devoted to telling it. But length and detail alone do not account for the fascination it has held for Bible readers through the centuries. Its importance lies, rather, in the way in which Joseph's life gives a detailed illustration of the sovereign purposes and wonderful providence of God.

Too often, books on the historical parts of Scripture are either dull or fanciful interpretations of the text. *The Life of Joesph*, by contrast, provides exposition that is both rich and warm. It also applies in a practical way the great principles of God's grace illustrated in Joseph's life. Reading it will confirm Spurgeon's enthusiastic comment that George Lawson was 'a man of great genius who had a heart alive both to the human and divine side of truth. Lawson wrote popularly and vigorously. . .'

George Lawson (1749-1820) was one of the outstanding preachers of the Scottish Secession Church. He served as his denomination's Professor of Divinity from 1787 until his death in 1820, combining his teaching duties with his pastoral ministry in Selkirk. His best known works were his 'Lectures' (the old Scots word for expositions), which were published during his lifetime. His study of the life of Joseph was the first of these.

ISBN 0 85151 161 9
576pp. Cloth-bound

IN THE BEGINNING
E.J. Young

In 1967 in the last year of his life, E.J. Young delivered in Toronto a series of popular addresses which are here reprinted. He had already published more than one book on this same section of Scripture but the forceful, spoken-style of these pages, and the simplicity with which he presents his final thoughts on the key issue in Genesis 1-3, makes this one of the most readable and important of all his writings. Nothing was of greater concern to him than that the Church should speak plainly and boldly on the inspired record of man's creation and fall and he demonstrates how a full acceptance of the divine authority of the Bible is essential to the proper interpretation of the Genesis narrative.

Dr Young taught the Old Testament at Westminster Theological Seminary, Philadelphia, from 1936 until his death on February 18, 1968. 'He knew nothing', wrote his colleague, John Murray, 'of an antithesis between devotion to the Lord and devotion to the Bible. He revered the Bible because he revered the Author.'

ISBN 0 85151 235 6
118pp. Paperback

A COMMENTARY ON GENESIS

John Calvin

Calvin is recognised, by common consent, as the greatest Biblical commentator of all time. He was also the pioneer of those principles of sound exegesis and genuine exposition which have been adopted by later writers. Although, when it was published in 1554, Genesis was not the first of Calvin's commentaries to have appeared, it is of outstanding importance because the book of Genesis is in every way fundamental to the interpretation of the whole Bible.

Because Calvin was a sound exegete, little of what he wrote is dated. Although his treatment of the early chapters is thorough, it is not disproportionate, and the later narratives concerning Noah, Abraham, Isaac, Jacob and Joseph are not passed over hastily. Indeed, Calvin excels in bringing out the principles of God's dealings with men, as individuals and in covenant, and in showing faithfully yet tenderly the human weakness and sin all too evident in Genesis.

ISBN 0 85151 093 0
1088pp. Cloth-bound

For a free illustrated catalogue please write to:
THE BANNER OF TRUTH TRUST
3 Murrayfield Road, Edinburgh EH12 6EL
P.O. Box 621, Carlisle, Pennsylvania, 17013, U.S.A.